Praise for *We're i̶* T0011707

A *Kirkus Reviews* Best Middle Grade Book of 2022
A *School Library Journal* Best Nonfiction Book of 2022

★ "The moments of accomplishment, struggle, sadness, and perseverance shown here provide a touching, uplifting image of America that is seldom represented. Equal parts inspiring, emotional, and informative: a necessary read."
—*Kirkus Reviews*, starred review

★ "Filled with information and insight, this young readers edition of the book *We Are Not Here to Be Bystanders* will inspire and motivate readers. . . . An excellent read that practically dares readers to take on the tough issues with strength and vigor, this is an outstanding purchase for all libraries."
—*School Library Journal*, starred review

"Sarsour's readable and uplifting story will empower young people in their own fight for social justice." —*Booklist*

Praise for *We Are Not Here to Be Bystanders*

"Sarsour's memoir is packed with hard-learned lessons from the front lines of the social-justice struggle. It's a book that speaks to our times." —*Washington Post*

"Candid and poignant, this book offers an intimate portrait of a committed activist while emphasizing the need for more Americans to work against the deep-seated inequalities that still haunt the country. A powerful memoir from a dedicated fighter for social justice." —*Kirkus Reviews*

"An incredible, galvanizing story of the power of participation."
—*Booklist*

ALSO BY LINDA SARSOUR

We Are Not Here to Be Bystanders

WE'RE
IN THIS
TOGETHER

A YOUNG READERS EDITION OF *WE ARE NOT HERE TO BE BYSTANDERS*

LINDA SARSOUR

SALAAM
READS

NEW YORK   LONDON   TORONTO   SYDNEY   NEW DELHI

SALAAM
R E A D S

An imprint of Simon & Schuster Children's Publishing Division
1230 Avenue of the Americas, New York, New York 10020
This work is a memoir. It reflects the author's present recollections of her experiences over a period of years.
Text © 2020, 2022 by Linda Sarsour
This young readers edition is adapted from *We Are Not Here to Be Bystanders* by Linda Sarsour
Cover illustration © 2022 by Petra Ericksson
Cover design by Krista Vossen © 2022 by Simon & Schuster, Inc.
All rights reserved, including the right of reproduction in whole or in part in any form.
SALAAM READS and its logo are trademarks of Simon & Schuster, Inc.
For information about special discounts for bulk purchases, please contact Simon & Schuster Special Sales at 1-866-506-1949 or business@simonandschuster.com.
The Simon & Schuster Speakers Bureau can bring authors to your live event. For more information or to book an event, contact the Simon & Schuster Speakers Bureau at 1-866-248-3049 or visit our website at www.simonspeakers.com.
Also available in a Salaam Reads hardcover edition
Interior design by Hilary Zarycky
The text for this book was set in New Caledonia LT Std.
Manufactured in the United States of America
0923 OFF
First Salaam Reads paperback edition October 2023
2   4   6   8   10   9   7   5   3   1
Library of Congress Control Number: 2022009856
ISBN 978-1-5344-3929-0 (hc)
ISBN 978-1-5344-3930-6 (pbk)
ISBN 978-1-5344-3931-3 (ebook)

To young students everywhere: I see you, I believe in you, and always remember, we're in this together.

Contents

CHAPTER 1

The Women's March

Signs danced above an ocean of people like boats bobbing on the sea. White signs, red signs, black signs, pink signs, proclaiming beautiful messages of unity.

LOVE TRUMPS HATE, declared a white sign with rainbow-colored letters.

WE THE PEOPLE ARE GREATER THAN FEAR, black letters on a yellow placard pronounced.

FIGHT LIKE A GIRL! shouted the pink letters beneath a picture of a red fist cradled by a garland of green.

On a January morning in 2017, I stood backstage during the Women's March on Washington. Under a silver sky, with the cool breeze at my face, I saw a pink expanse spread before me in every direction, a patchwork quilt of baby pink, blush, neon pink, fuchsia. I could hear women talking to one another in a low hum, but their signs shouted their messages loudly.

WHEN THEY GO LOW, WE GO HIGH!

THE FUTURE IS FEMALE!

Where did all these women come from? I wondered.

I imagined mothers and daughters, sisters and sister-friends, classmates and coworkers from all over the country days earlier. In my mind's eye I saw them gathered in kitchens over pizza and soda, or spread out on the carpet on living room floors. I heard them conversing with one another.

"What do you want to say on your poster?"

"Dump Trump!"

"No. Why not something more positive about the society we want to create?"

I imagined them thoughtfully penciling their messages onto poster board, contemplating their favorite colors, and then carefully coloring in the letters. Even from the stage, I could smell the sharp odor of the markers.

This was the morning I'd been waiting for. The morning that we, the women of the United States and our allies, would stand up against the forces of hate and division and make our voices heard.

But I gotta be honest: even as one of the organizers, I was stunned by how many women already stood on Independence Avenue at the southwest corner of the United States Capitol grounds. I turned my head to the left and saw people crammed down the side streets. To the right people were sandwiched into those roads as well. Some women even had babies swaddled to their chests, the babies' cheeks as bright as the knit caps that had become the signature look of the march. Behind the crowd, the Capitol gleamed white with the promise of democracy.

One of my closest friends, Tamika Mallory, walked over. "What time is it?"

"It's like eight fifteen," I answered.

"There are so many people that I can't see the back of the crowd!" she exclaimed.

Tamika was one of my besties. Over the years, together with our friend Carmen Perez, we had supported each other more times than we could count as we'd fought for justice and equality for everyone. We were so close that we could read each other's minds. Some people had begun to think of us as a social justice Voltron, so-called after the 1980s cartoon featuring a group of teens who teamed up to build and pilot a robot, Voltron, that defends the universe.

Just three months earlier the Voltron and fashion designer Bob Bland had been named one of the march's lead organizers, back when the event had been just an idea dancing in our collective imagination. At that point we had been determined and passionate but uncertain about whether our idea for the march would work. Now a seemingly endless expanse of people stretched before us.

Together Tamika and I walked toward the front of the stage.

Directly ahead, a girl with caramel skin, probably eight years old, sat on her mother's shoulders. The girl wore a cameo-pink hat and a coral-pink shirt with the word *LOVE* written simply with a marker. A sign with the words THE FUTURE IS FEMALE danced on the crowd beside her.

Then a new sound emerged. It began toward the back of the crowd as a low hum. But it grew louder as it rolled forward, a sonic wave. When it finally reached the front of the throng, the force of the energy filled my heart and wrapped around me like a huge hug of love.

"ARRRRR!"

The banners danced in rhythm with the sound.

HEAR ME ROAR! one of the signs exclaimed.

The people immediately in front of the stage started whooping, jumping up and down, waving, clapping, and shouting. Brown people, tan people, white people; women wearing pink hijabs; women with pink headwraps twisted high on their heads; blond women, redheads; women with spiky hair. We, the women of the United States of America!

Suddenly I realized that they had recognized us and were cheering for us! My arms and legs tingled with goose bumps.

"We did this!" Tamika whispered into my ear as her arm reached around and hugged me.

A smile took over my face as I waved back to the crowd.

It was at that moment that I noticed the most amazing sight of all: the march's signature sign of a Muslim American woman wearing the red, white, and blue American flag wrapped around her head and shoulders as her hijab.

I was a child of Muslim American immigrants and a member of a community that had been constantly vilified for many years, and this was the most beautiful sight I'd ever seen.

My entire life had prepared me for this moment. I felt fire leap inside my belly. Today I would stand up to bullying; I would no longer feel "less than"; I would stand in front of the world as a symbol of strength.

I would speak with the authority that all these women

who had traveled to our nation's seat of power were giving me. I would speak about creating a society by the people and for the people. I prayed that God would give me the right words—words that were truthful, words that inspired, words that empowered.

But much remained to be done over the next several hours. Tamika and I waved, then turned and left the stage to finish preparing for the march.

My time onstage would come.

CHAPTER 2

Journey to the American Dream

I haven't spent my life standing on stages. I'm the proud daughter of a working-class family of immigrants and grew up in Brooklyn, New York. My parents came to the US from Palestine in the 1970s. Both had grown up learning and dreaming of this peaceful place called America—the "land of the free" that they had seen on TV.

Living in a nation that had been ravaged by war, my father's family had encouraged him to come here since he was a young boy. My dad's name is Nidal. In Arabic it means "to struggle and fight in defense," but my father is actually a cheerful soul. Yaba, as we call him, is extremely outgoing, the life of the party. He's tall and gangly, friendly and loud; you can always hear my father coming. He wears his emotions on his sleeve. His laugh booms—he has an irrepressible sense of humor. Everyone calls him Nick—actually, Crazy Nick!

Yaba arrived in the US in 1976, joining his brother

Mohammad, who had already immigrated to Brooklyn. My father worked alongside his brother at a small bodega—a corner store—there. My mother joined my father three years later. Unlike Yaba, my mother is very tiny. She is barely five feet tall, has tan skin, dresses modestly, and covers her hair with a hijab. She is quite reserved and emotionally can be hard to read.

As a couple they embody the phrase "opposites attract." But despite their differences, they pursued a common dream, to live in a place where you could be whoever you wanted to be, worship whatever god you believed in, and work hard and experience abundance. They imagined having a family here. Before long, they had me, followed by my four sisters, and then, several years later, my two brothers, DJ and Mo, born exactly one year apart.

In the years before my brothers were born, my family lived in a small one-bedroom apartment in Brooklyn. And I will never forget the day when the landlord came knocking. I was only seven years old at the time, but old enough that my parents let me answer the front door. I was proud that they trusted me with that responsibility. After I stood on a chair and looked out through the peephole, I opened the door.

"Hello!" I greeted the landlord as Lena, Heeba, Hanady, and Hela ran to line up behind me, from biggest to smallest, each just one or two years apart.

"Who are these children?" he asked as the baby, Hela, crawled across the hardwood floor to join us.

"These are my sisters," I told him proudly, as the oldest. "This is Lena, this—"

"Your *sisters*?" he interrupted, his voice sharp, and then his mouth gaped open. "This is a one-and-a-half-bedroom apartment!" he yelled.

I froze in the face of his angry energy and didn't know what to say.

Once my mother heard the commotion, she came racing from the bedroom, straightening her modest blue dress.

"I am so s-sorry, sir," Yumma stuttered, struggling with her English.

"You can't have all these children living here," he huffed. "This is against the rules."

"So sorry, sir," she repeated. I noticed her shoulders drooping, her eyes blinking back tears, and her hands wringing.

I desperately wanted to help my mother, but I felt overwhelmed by this angry man, and I didn't understand what was wrong or know what to do.

"You can't stay here with all these children," he told her. "Do you understand?"

"Yes, sir," she said.

As the oldest, I felt ashamed for my mother and wondered if I had done something wrong. My mother was always so careful in the apartment. "Don't run, don't yell," she would tell us when we would color, play with dolls, or play games like hide-and-seek with one another. Maybe this was my fault.

"I'm sorry, Yumma," I told my mother after the landlord had gone, barely able to raise my teary eyes to meet hers as I remembered moments when maybe we'd laughed too loudly.

"Don't worry, Linda," she told me as she pulled me close. "This isn't your fault."

Even with Yumma's reassurances, I wasn't so certain.

The world in a small town

Sometimes a bad moment can lead to a good one.

After the incident with the landlord, my parents purchased a three-story, three-bedroom town house in Sunset Park, the highest point in all of Brooklyn.

Our house was a fixer-upper, as Yaba would say. Even though my father had to spend a lot of time fixing the house, there were benefits to moving. For one, we had a lot more space. Now we had more room to play and grow. I shared a bedroom with my younger sister Lena. After so many years of being all squeezed together, I had some space to myself.

In time my parents repaired the exterior of our home with linoleum siding. Yumma picked out the color—a very bright yellow. And when I say "bright," I don't mean a pastel. I mean bright-bright.

Lemon yellow.

Canary yellow.

Sunshine yellow.

Banana yellow.

People called our house the banana-boat house. When I was little, I didn't mind. But the older I got, the more mortified I became. To this day, I'm still embarrassed. The rest of our block looked a lot more normal, with homes in darker colors.

My life was very stereotypically Brooklyn in the late 1980s and '90s. The entire world lived in our not-so-small town. Brooklyn is this really amazing place full of people who are from over one hundred forty countries and who speak over one hundred seventy languages. There are communities full of immigrants from Mexico, the Middle East, China, Nigeria, the Philippines, Russia, Jamaica, and more.

On our block the family to our left was from Ecuador; the family on our right was from Yemen. Across the street was another Palestinian family. People from Mexico, Honduras, the Philippines, and Puerto Rico were also repped on my block. One thing my neighborhood friends had in common with me was that none of our parents spoke fluent English. Which meant we all grew up bilingual or even trilingual!

"Yumma, guess what happened today," I'd say after a long day at school.

"Stop, Linda," Yumma would answer. "Please tell me in Arabic."

It was important to my mother that I be fully bilingual and proud of my Palestinian and American heritage. My friends and I would slide back and forth between languages as the situation required. On our street you would not merely witness a mosaic of humanity but also hear the symphony of our languages.

With all of us kids playing in the concrete area in front of our home, our house became the neighborhood gathering place. And what a gathering place it was! With my family of nine, once my two brothers were born, the Yemeni family of nine, and the Palestinian family of nine, there were always about twenty-five kids at our home.

Amazingly, the kids in the other families were ages similar to me and my siblings. So each of us automatically had two friends just from those two other families.

Friendship found us right on our block.

Our mothers would gossip, exchange parenting advice, share dishes and recipes—from stuffed grape leaves to empanadas—and get the hang of the ins and outs of their new nation. Every mom on our street had permission to scold me, call me in, or call me out if I got out of line. It would never even have occurred to me to tattle, "The lady up the street just yelled at me."

"You must have deserved it," my mom would have said. That's how much trust they had in one another.

On hot summer afternoons we would play Wiffle ball and tag. Then, inevitably, someone would open the water hydrants, and all of us Black, Brown, and beige kids would swarm the street and run through the spray. Then our moms would call us in for dinner. Our street was a place of youthful innocence and pure joy.

As the years roll by, old customs and memories can slip from your hands as easily as a dream dissipates when you awaken.

So my parents and our immigrant neighbors tried both to be American and to hold on to the cultural values of the worlds they'd left behind.

With hindsight, I can see that those beliefs were surprisingly similar. Even though our families came from different places, we shared many of the same cultural values.

Listen to your elders.

Speak with respect.

Do what your parents tell you to do.

When our moms called us inside, we didn't roll our eyes, or ask for "five minutes more," or say "I'll come in in a little while." We just stopped what we were doing and went inside. Even if we were in the middle of an intense game of tag, none of the other kids thought it was weird that the game had to stop so we could go home.

Our parents, uncertain about their language skills and the rules in this new country, wanted us to experience the world but also wanted to protect us and hold us close. They didn't let us go far except to take the bus or train to and from school. Though we all had to be home by three fifteen, sometimes we'd be late.

"Oh, shoot. It's ten after three!" Lena would say.

"Hurry up so we don't get in trouble!" I'd yell as we raced up the hill.

My main source of pure joy was Sunset Park, the actual park our neighborhood was named for, located just one block away. Filled with swings, slides, a soccer field, a swimming pool, volleyball nets, a handball court, and the Police Athletic League—a sanctuary offering after-school programs and basketball leagues—the park brimmed with kids of all colors, creeds, and cultural backgrounds. We didn't need to know one another's names or even speak the same languages; we just had a natural attraction to play with each other.

Though there was so much to do, my favorite memories are of playing tag.

This little patch of heaven was a godsend for my mom. Because let's be honest—there is no way that one mother can watch seven children at a playground. The moms cared for one another's children as their own. Yumma could sit with her friends and know her kids were safe, even in those moments when she couldn't quite see us.

Many evenings we would lay a blanket across the green stretches of grass and admire the way the sun would leave streaks the colors of sunflower, deep rose, and tangerine behind the World Trade Center, the Empire State Building, and other skyscrapers in Manhattan whose lights flickered a few miles across the bay.

Back then it really felt like we'd achieved my parents' American dream.

CHAPTER 3

A Village within a Village

As I bounded up the stoop on my way home from school, I could smell what my mother was cooking before I even entered the house. The fragrance of ground lamb simmering in seven-spice—a combination of cinnamon, cardamom, cumin, black coriander, cloves, paprika, and black pepper—was the only clue I needed. I knew that she was making waraqa dawali, or grape leaves stuffed with rice and meat.

"Yumma, my favorite," I said, reaching to pick a stuffed grape leaf out of the dish where she had carefully stacked them.

"No, Linda," she told me. "You need to wash your hands when you come into the house."

I ran to the bathroom and lathered with Ivory soap, then tasted one of these sumptuous treats.

When I was twelve, Yumma had taught me how to make

grape leaves. She'd shown me how to soak the rice, season the meat, and simmer it slowly so it wouldn't overcook, how to not add the salt too early. I'd learned how to carefully lay the dark green leaves out on the chopping block so I could drop a dollop of rice and lamb inside them, then carefully roll them up, coat them in olive oil, and decorate them with lemon slices.

My mother's waraqa dawali were a hit every time our family attended a wedding, graduation, birthday celebration, engagement party, or fundraiser for Palestine held by anyone in the sizeable community of Palestinians who lived in Sunset Park. In fact, my parents had basically emigrated from a small Palestinian village called El Bireh to a village of Palestinians living in Brooklyn. Aunts, uncles, cousins, and neighbors from my parents' hometown gathered together often. One of my mother's brothers, Bassam, taught us Palestinian folkloric dancing, with her other brother, Talal, playing the shibbabeh, a short flute. My sisters and I mastered the quick, intricate footwork of dabka so well that we even formed an official dabka dance troupe that, for a while, was in great demand at social events. (I even taught Palestinian folkloric dancing at a dance studio as an adult.)

Though they weren't very religious—my mom still did salat, praying five times a day—my parents made sure we learned about Islam. The word "Islam" comes from the Arabic word "peace," which is a central tenet of the Islamic faith. In fact, many Muslims greet each other saying, "Assalamu Alaikum!" or "Peace be upon you." The response, "Wa Alaikum Salaam," means "And peace be upon you too."

Five Facts to Know about Islam

In the event that you're not familiar with Islam, here are some facts that you should know:

1. A Muslim practices Islam, just as a Jew practices Judaism and a Christian practices Christianity.

2. Islam is the second-largest religion in the world, following Christianity. There are almost 2 billion Muslims worldwide, including nearly 3.5 million in North America. In more than fifty countries the majority of the population is Muslim. It is the world's fastest-growing religion.[1]

3. Muslims read the Qur'an, a book filled with sacred wisdom and teachings. It is written in Arabic. Sometimes "Qur'an" is spelled "Koran."

4. Located in Saudi Arabia, Mecca is Islam's birthplace and holiest city. Each year millions of Muslims travel to Mecca to fulfill one of the pillars of Islam. This journey is called hajj. Sometimes Mecca is spelled "Makkah."

5. Muslims pray five times a day—before sunrise, at noon, in the afternoon, at sunset, and in the evening. All prayers are performed facing Mecca. Islam has five central beliefs and practices: professing your faith, praying, charity, fasting, and making the pilgrimage to Mecca.[2]

On Saturdays and Sundays, I attended Islamic school with my siblings and about fifty other kids. From the time I was eight until I turned sixteen, I learned to read and write Arabic; I memorized and recited verses from the Qur'an, Islam's holy book; and I learned the values of my faith. I learned that Islam is an expression of love, devotion to family, service to others, and the pursuit of fairness and truth. We would make hundreds of cheese sandwiches and hand them out to homeless people in Times Square and at various train stations to express some of Islam's most important tenets: compassion and giving to others. We'd water plants and plant flowers and trees in the parks to show our reverence to God by taking care of the earth and its blessings.

Beginning when I was seven years old, I would fast from dawn to sunset every year during Ramadan. For me, Ramadan meant a lot of family dinners. My parents would invite a different family over every night—my aunt's family, our neighbors across the street, my dad's employees and their families, and so on. Every evening we would break our fast with twenty or thirty people. I looked forward to going to mosque and being part of the community.

We also celebrated the Islamic holidays Eid al-Fitr and Eid al-Adha. During Eid, children receive money as gifts. Between all my aunts and uncles, I might end up with $150. Consistent with the value of zakat, which refers to charity, we were taught to give a percentage of our money and possessions to people less fortunate than us. At one point my dad sponsored a girl named Zoya, in Ethiopia, through the Save the Children organization. Ethiopia was experiencing extreme famine at the time, and while I don't recall all the details of her life, I do remember that she had sisters and that their father had passed away. Each month we would receive a progress report to tell us how Zoya was doing. The fact that our dad was helping to take care of her made it feel like she was our sister.

Some Islamic Holidays and Their Significance

Eid al-Adha

Eid al-Adha (pronounced "eed-uhl-ad-HA") is one of the biggest holidays in Islam. It reminds us to trust in God during the hard times in our lives. Eid al-Adha is celebrated with a huge feast. Children receive gifts.

Eid al-Fitr

Once a year Muslims participate in a spiritual practice called a fast. During this fast (known as Ramadan) we do not eat or drink during daylight hours. This fast reminds us to focus on God. It also helps us learn discipline and patience. At the end of the fast, we celebrate with a huge feast, a holiday called Eid al-Fitr (pronounced "eed-uhl-fit-er").

I was deeply touched by the impact my father was able to make for twenty-three dollars a month, so I chose to use my money to do something similar.

Just a few weeks later, I walked into the kitchen after school and gave my mom a hug, as I always did.

"Here, this is for you," she told me in Arabic, handing me an envelope that had been sitting on the counter.

It was big and fat. I was curious because I didn't often receive mail. I opened it, careful not to give myself a paper cut. It contained a manila folder. Inside the folder was a photograph of a gorgeous, slender Brown girl with big beautiful eyes that stared back at me. I read the letter that came with the picture. It said her name was Abebah; she was eight years old; it described her life and things she liked. I had contributed to her life. Now, in my mind, she too was my sister.

It made a tremendous impression on me to see that my twenty-three dollars had bought her a new pair of shoes, helped her get immunized, and improved her life. Every few months when our Save the Children envelope came, my sisters and I would gather around the table excitedly.

"Look what a difference you are making," our parents would tell us. "Look at how God has blessed you with the things you have. Now you are blessing others."

But these types of interactions also raised difficult questions.

"Why doesn't everyone have what we have?" we would ask.

"Because God is testing your character, your faith and resilience," they would tell us. "He gives some to you, and you give some to others."

This was my parents' Islam in action.

Week after week I would see the same Palestinian American people over and over. While it was great to have our community, sometimes my parents would still feel a little homesick.

For my mother, interacting with so many folks from El Bireh helped assuage her heartache and keep cherished memories and feelings of home from fading away with time and distance. These relationships also helped her hold on to valued traditions and cultural norms, and impart them to us much more easily. Even before I traveled to Palestine for the first time, I felt like it was already a part of me.

Every winter my grandparents would send us olives and olive oil. My parents experienced so much joy receiving the boxes, opening them, and carefully removing the two-liter Pepsi bottles filled with the golden-green elixir. They would bond while unwrapping the tape that sealed the bottles shut, smelling the oil, and pouring a little bit into a glass and tasting it. The light in their eyes, the glee in their hearts, the brightness in their spirits spilled over onto all of us like warm olive oil. When they were homesick and lonely, the olives and oil helped soothe them.

The life of the party

My father normally worked Monday through Saturday from seven in the morning to nine at night, so he didn't have a lot of personal friends. But every other weekend our entire extended family would go to Sunday-afternoon cookouts at my uncle Naji's house.

I could never predict exactly who from our sprawling clan might show up for these gatherings, but there was one person I looked for most of all—my cousin Basemah Atweh.

I was never really sure whether Basemah was my second cousin or third. Palestinians don't much care about those kinds of distinctions. We call our elders "auntie" or "uncle," whether we are blood relatives or not. A cousin is a cousin. Nobody cares whether you are literally a relative, so our families tend to be large and expansive.

Basemah had grown up with my father in the West Bank of Palestine, but she was my mother's age and one of her closest friends. I'd played with her son from the time we were young.

Click, click, click!

You could always hear her strutting up the walkway in her signature kitten heels before you'd see her, dressed in a perfect jewel-colored outfit with a matching bag. I would rush out to greet her. Basemah was the life of the party. Like Yaba's, her personality was big and loud, and energized any room. I loved to see her laugh more than almost anything else in the world. She laughed so hard that she could barely breathe. It was almost as if she were having an asthma attack. Of course, everyone would laugh along, just to share in her joy.

Cousin Basemah was a role model in many ways. Tall and heavyset with creamy white skin even lighter than mine, she didn't look very much like how many people imagine an Arab woman looks. Rather than keeping her hair its natural dark color, Basemah would dye her dark hair blond. Unlike many of her peers, she didn't cover it, and she wore her hair salon-coiffed. Her lipstick was bright red or pink or purple to go with her clothes, and her manicured nails matched perfectly. Her eyelashes were long, thick, and dark; her eyes were lined with kohl.

"Basemah, how come you never wear the same thing twice?" I'd ask. She walked in like she knew she was special.

And she was.

Women would flock to Basemah, marveling. In a conservative community and era—one in which women were supposed to make themselves small and not take up too much room—Basemah's confidence dominated any space she was in. She enjoyed and appreciated every inch of her ample figure, and she inspired people around her to enjoy and appreciate themselves too. Everything glowed a little brighter and felt more hopeful around her.

"I don't take crap from anybody, and you shouldn't either," she'd tell us cheerfully. She was one tough cookie; a jolly, conspiratorial big sister.

Every person who met her ended up adoring her, and it wasn't just because of her bubbly personality. You knew within minutes that Basemah would support you in any battle you might need help fighting. I would lean into her strength as I grew older. And little did I know then that one day in the future, she would ask for assistance from me.

CHAPTER 4

The Bodega

Way back when I was four years old, my father bought and opened a bodega in Crown Heights, a predominately Black and Latinx section of Brooklyn. He named it Linda Sarsour's Spanish & American Food Center. Back then it was very unusual for an Arab man to name a business after a daughter; Arab men usually named things after their firstborn sons. But Yaba had been extremely euphoric about my birth. When his friends would question him about the name of the store, he'd say, "Why should I wait? Linda is everything to me. Why shouldn't I celebrate her as I would a boy?"

So, Linda Sarsour's operated from Monday through Sunday, from dawn until long after dusk. For much of my childhood I only saw my dad on Sundays, his one day off. He would be gone before I woke up during the week and wouldn't come home until after I was asleep. Sometimes as I snuggled under the covers, I would promise myself that I would wake up the next morning in time to see him.

That never worked.

With my father at the store for such long hours and with so many children to raise, most of my mother's work centered on our home. She was a mother and a housewife, and supported the family business. When we were young, a lot of her responsibilities related to babies and young children—changing diapers, bottles, feedings. Practicing Palestinian artistry in the kitchen for nine hungry mouths meant that her grocery runs would take two or three hours. Laundry and cleaning would take much longer. And when you own a bodega, you handle a lot of cash. My mom made sure it made it to the bank.

As the oldest, I would help dress, feed, and babysit my siblings. I'd also assist around the house. I would cut notepaper into little pieces, write the name of one room—living room, dining room, kitchen, bathroom—on each, fold them into tiny balls, and then have my sisters pick the papers out of a bowl. Whatever room you pulled was what you were cleaning that day. I would walk around overseeing the process, making sure my siblings used the right products and that everything was spotless.

One day Lena started eyeing me suspiciously.

"Hold up! How do you not get a room to clean?" she asked.

"Someone has to be the organizer," I told her.

Only God knew that I had spoken my future!

My mom, she thought it was hilarious that it had taken so long for my sisters to figure out what I'd been doing. The mischievous twinkle in her eyes told me, *You are onto something!*

I've been organizing people ever since.

Sometimes the seeds of the things you'll be good at when you're older get planted, grow roots, and even sprout when you're young.

Over the years, I did a lot of fending for myself, learning to navigate back and forth between my world at home, flavored with our Palestinian cultural traditions, and the mainstream American society, I often served as translator, particularly for my mom. I filled out school forms, made sure that my siblings completed their homework before going outside to play, and signed everyone's school permission slips. To spare her frustration and embarrassment, I helped Yumma communicate in English with our teachers, the pediatrician, the people in the billing office at the utility company. The fact that I played so many roles made learning particularly important to me.

Our lives tied together

When I turned twelve, I started working at the bodega after school on Tuesdays and Thursdays as Yaba's cashier. Mom would pick me up from school in her red Lincoln Navigator and drive me the twenty-five minutes to the store, located at the intersection of Troy Avenue and Montgomery Street. So I grew up in Crown Heights as much as in Sunset Park.

Everyone came to Yaba's bodega: African Americans, Caribbean and Central American immigrants, Puerto Ricans, and a few Orthodox Jews. The store was a neighborhood gathering place. Sometimes people would come to shop; other times they would just stop by to bring my father up to speed on what was going on in their lives. When you were with my father, even if you weren't in the mood to laugh, you had to laugh, because his laugh made you laugh, so people liked to stop by. Yaba would converse with customers, chat with the postman, sit outside on stacked milk crates and shoot the breeze with the people who lived above the store, and chitchat with neighbors as they walked by. When I was a little older, and his business was better established, he would take the time to sip Turkish coffee with some of the many other Arab men who owned bodegas. His personal life took place at work because sixteen-hour days didn't leave time for having many friends at home.

I greeted people and rang up their purchases while I did my homework. I got to know all the neighborhood kids as they bought milk, bread, toilet paper, kosher goods. Sometimes a kid didn't have enough cash. My father taught me to dutifully write their parents' names in the marbled composition notebooks where he recorded the credit he extended to his regular customers. Their parents would pay their debts when payday came or less meager times arrived. Sometimes our Orthodox Jewish customers would need to buy something after sundown on the Sabbath, when their religion didn't allow them to handle money. Other times people's money would just run short and they'd need my dad to float them. Yaba never worried about when the ledgers would be squared. He appreciated his customers. They paid what they could, a little at a time, until their debts were gone, and Yaba trusted them with a simplicity that moved me, even as a young girl. In the process of interacting with so many different people, I learned that even though people may look very different, every human being has very similar wants and needs.

Deep ties

I remember one afternoon gazing out the bodega window, watching kids from the public school across the way being rowdy at the bus stop. My dad stood next to me as a skinny African American boy, who couldn't have been more than twelve, entered the store and walked past us, his hair cropped so close to his head that it was hardly more than a shadow. The boy walked to the coolers in the back where the sodas and twenty-five-cent juices were. Then he selected a juice as well as a twenty-five-cent Hostess lemon cake from a display rack. The kid looked around, trying to make sure the store shelves blocked him from our view, and then he tucked the juice box and cake into the pockets of his jacket. He didn't realize that Yaba could see him in a large circular mirror that offered a fun-house view of the four long aisles of the store. The boy then walked to the front of the store, pushed the glass door open, and left.

Yaba followed him outside. "Jerome," he said, "please give me what's in your pockets."

The boy spun around, looking stricken. I don't think he'd realized that Yaba knew his name. "I—I—I don't have any-thing in my p-p-pockets," he stammered.

"Don't lie to me, son," Yaba responded calmly. "I saw you

put that quarter juice and quarter cake in your pocket. Now give them to me."

Jerome placed the items he'd stolen into my father's hand.

"Why did you steal these things?" Yaba asked, sounding disappointed, almost hurt. "I know your mother. She didn't raise you to do something reckless like this. What do you think she would say if I told her what you did?"

"She's at work," Jerome mumbled, his voice so soft that I barely caught the words. "I didn't have any money."

"Stay right here," Yaba told him. "You don't move."

Then he came inside, placed the quarter juice and little cake into a brown paper bag, and folded the top down. He went back outside and handed the bag to Jerome, stooping down so that he was at eye level.

"The next time you are hungry and don't have any money, you don't steal what you want," Yaba told him. "You come in here and you ask me, and I will give it to you. Do you understand?"

Jerome nodded vigorously, his eyes filling with tears. Yaba patted him on the shoulder and stood watching as he turned and ran off down the block, clutching the bag. Then my father walked back into his store and said nothing more.

Years later it would occur to me that Yaba could have called the police on Jerome, but that would have resulted in Jerome's having a police record. Yaba truly cared about his customers, and they cared about him. My many hours in the store taught me that my life, well-being, and experiences were deeply tied to my community.

Yaba's business provided amply for our family. We weren't

rich, but our family never needed food stamps, publicly funded healthcare, or any help from the government. With the earnings from our bodega, my father was able to buy one of his favorite possessions—an enormous twelve-passenger burgundy Chevy Suburban with matching velvet curtains on the windows. With three rows of passenger seats plus a back row that folded down into a bed, the car looked like the stretch limos that transport celebrities to the red carpet. But it held our sprawling family comfortably when we traveled the four hours to Boston to visit my uncle Mohammad. Yaba also owned a work car, a two-door silver Monte Carlo. Each time he pressed the horn, it played a loud melody. On weekends he would beep the horn at the top of our street, alerting the whole neighborhood that he was coming.

Yaba and Yumma believed that we were a part of the American dream. They valued the fact that their children were receiving a free public education, something particularly important since their own educations had been disrupted. My parents believed this country had given them everything they had, and God had blessed us, and we had enough.

CHAPTER 5

Palestine

One day when I was in eighth grade, our social studies teacher divided the class into different groups. We were to research a country and create a poster board with maps and facts. My group was assigned Australia.

Four of us sat at a table—a Haitian American girl named Chantal, who was one of my best friends; a kid named Carlos, whom I didn't know very well and had joined our class just that year; an African American boy named Jalal; and me.

"Hey, Carlos, where's your family from?" I asked as I positioned tracing paper over a page in an atlas and began to draw the outline of Australia.

"My mom's Puerto Rican and my dad's Dominican," he said.

"Hey, Linda, where's *your* family from?" Jalal asked.

"We're from Palestine," I responded.

I loved attending such diverse schools, but the fact that

so many of the Palestinian kids in my community attended Muslim schools left me to grapple with my identity without other students like me. Few teachers, not to mention children, understood my background, so I pretty much knew what would come next.

"Palestine?" Jalal said. "What's that?"

I went into my usual explanation—the Middle East, the Holy Land where Jesus walked, the whole nine yards. Jalal, Chantal, and Carlos looked at me in a curious way. I could tell that none of them had ever heard of my family's homeland. Then Jalal, who had a lively, bubbly personality, jumped up from his chair and stood in front of the huge map of the world that hung on the wall right by the table. His fingers traveled over mountains and oceans and came to rest on the Middle East.

"Where's Palestine at?" he asked. "I see Syria," he said, stabbing the map with his finger. "I see Jordan and Israel, but I don't see Palestine here. Where do you see Palestine?"

He was right. Palestine was *not* on the map. I sighed and went back to tracing the coastline of Australia.

"Hey, Linda, I don't see no Palestine on this map," Jalal continued. Now in jokester mode, he wouldn't let it go. "You sure you're really from there? How come I never heard of it?"

"You know, there was a war, and a lot of problems happened there," I mumbled, a sinking feeling developing in my midsection. Then I decided I was not going to go down this road again. Not today. Jalal wasn't trying to be mean; clearly he didn't understand how much his teasing hurt as he experimented with different comedic voices, repeating, "Where you see Palestine at? I don't see no Palestine. Why they leave your country off this map, Linda?" His playful questions filled me with shame. I couldn't show I was from Palestine, or that such a place even existed.

"I don't know, Jalal," I said finally, feeling defeated, coloring Australia in with hard, furious crayon strokes. "Why don't you go ask the teacher?"

Something flickered across Jalal's face, as he was catching on that I didn't find this amusing. As Chantal moved next to me to help me color, he became lost studying the red-ink borders of the Middle East. I caught Carlos watching me, his face scrunched into a frown. I wondered if he thought I was lying. This exchange left me feeling shattered, but if you had asked me why, I wouldn't have been able to tell you.

The adventure ahead

Though I'd traveled to Palestine before, the first trip that I really remember occurred when I was eight.

"Why are we going again?" Yumma complained to Yaba. "It's not that serious."

"What are you talking about?" my father responded. "What if we don't go and something happens to your mom or my mom?"

"What if something happens here?"

"Don't worry," responded my father, an eternal optimist. "God will give us the money back."

This was how the journey began—with my mother worrying about the astronomical costs of nine people traveling to the Middle East, and Yaba being Yaba. Weeks in advance my parents would purchase new suitcases, buy gifts, and get our passports and papers in order.

Excited about the adventure ahead, I couldn't sleep well the night before. The travel day seemed like it lasted forever. We said our goodbyes to our neighbors and loaded into the Suburban so Uncle Naji could take us to Kennedy Airport. There we began the endless process of standing in line, lugging our bags to the counter, getting our tickets, walking through the terminal to our gate, sitting and waiting, and finally lining up on the Jetway to board the plane.

From New York most flights to the Middle East take off at about seven thirty p.m. and fly overnight.

I remember tuning my ear to the flight attendants, trying to understand their announcements, made in English, French, Hebrew, and Arabic. Sitting in the window seat, I felt both excited and anxious as the jet rumbled down the runway. After takeoff my siblings and I looked out the window at the spectacular sight of New York City from above.

"There's Brooklyn!"

"The Empire State Building's right over there."

"Is that the Chrysler Building?"

"Hey, there's the World Trade Center!"

Of course we looked for the landmark twin towers, which back then were some of the tallest buildings in the world. My parents would always point out the Statue of Liberty, which held tremendous significance for them.

We flew overnight, then landed at Charles de Gaulle Airport in Paris, France, at about nine the following morning. We got off the plane, stood in the line to go through customs, walked across the huge airport to the gate for our next flight, then sat down close to our gate to relax and find a place to eat breakfast.

It was thrilling to be in a different country, seeing signs written in French and English, and seeing so many people from around the world speaking different languages.

Three hours later we boarded a flight to Tel Aviv, Israel's second-largest city. I chatted with my sisters for a while, then dozed off.

"Time to wake up," Yumma said, nudging me as the plane began its descent.

"We're here," we shouted when the plane touched down, almost six thousand miles later, as all the passengers clapped and cheered.

An intimidating experience

Yaba suddenly became very tense.

"We are traveling in a new country now," he instructed us. "The laws here in Israel are different from the laws in the United States."

As we walked up the Jetway, my parents held my younger siblings' hands.

"No running," Yumma advised.

"Stay close," Yaba warned. "And do not say anything unless I say it's okay."

Then we exited the Jetway into Ben Gurion Airport.

It was as though we had stepped into a different world. Suddenly we were surrounded by many people wearing traditional Middle Eastern clothing—long tunics or black robes called thawbs, or the black abayas some women wore. Many more women were wearing hijabs here to cover their hair than they did back in Brooklyn. My mother, who sometimes stood out at home, blended right in. (My sisters and I didn't cover.) I heard people speaking English and Arabic, as well as other languages I wasn't familiar with.

Never before had I seen the men clad in desert boots and tan-camouflage military fatigues, holding machine guns and carrying automatic pistols on their hips. A few handled large German shepherds on leashes that would occasionally sniff people and their luggage. This caused my feet to stop moving.

"Yaba, why . . . ," I began, but Yumma grabbed my hand and yanked me forward.

"Now is not the time for questions, sweet Linda," Yaba replied. "Don't stare; just look straight ahead."

I followed his instructions, but my legs felt rubbery. Before long the crowd slowed, and we found ourselves standing in a line. In time a customs official in a security booth called us forward. My father handed the man all our passports.

"Name, please?" he demanded, using a tone that seemed disrespectful of Yaba's age.

"Nidal Sarsour."

"Is this your family?" he said, nodding toward the rest of us.

"Yes."

"Why are you here?"

"To visit my mother."

"How long will you be staying?"

"Four weeks."

"Where will you be?"

"In El Bireh, Palestine."

The customs official's eyes narrowed. "What is the reason for your trip?"

"To visit family."

"What is the exact location where you will be staying?"

The questions felt increasingly intrusive.

"Who will you be staying with? . . . What is their relationship to you?" The queries seemed endless.

Yumma's brow was furrowed, her skin pale, lips tight, and shoulders rounded. I looked at my shoes, the tiles on the floor, the German shepherd passing by from time to time—anywhere to keep from feeling shame for Yaba. After what seemed like forever, we were free to go. But though Yaba tried to pretend like everything was normal, he wasn't his usual booming self. We got our luggage and passed through two additional checkpoints, where soldiers searched our bags. Then we headed for the exit.

When we stepped outside, a bunch of families were laughing, hugging, and welcoming one another. I expected Sitty Sarah, Grandpa Ahmed, or one of my many cousins to greet us. But instead my father waved down a man whom he obviously knew, and we walked toward his van parked at the curb.

Resilience and resistance

A group of soldiers stopped the van as we were leaving the airport. Our driver handed over his papers, my father's ID, and our family's passports to one soldier as two others slowly walked around the car, inspecting it, peering beneath it, and staring at us through the windows. It was the first of several military checkpoints we navigated, causing a twenty-minute ride to El Bireh to take forty-five minutes.

Along the way we passed through a checkpoint at the Palestinian border, which was very tense as well. Crossing into Palestine made everyone feel relief.

I pressed my face to the window as we entered my parents' homeland. I watched men and women dressed in T-shirts and jeans, and a few in traditional Middle Eastern attire, walking down the street.

Finally we arrived in El Bireh. When Grandpa Atif came outside to greet us, Yumma burst into tears; so did my sisters and I.

"Why didn't you come to meet us at the airport?" I asked them.

Grandpa Atif looked at my parents knowingly before saying, "God willing, we will meet you there another time." Then he gently rubbed my head.

Later I'd discover that my family in Palestine wasn't permitted to enter Israel.

Modest and traditional

My grandparents lived in a modest traditional Palestinian house made from stone and sun-dried bricks, with a flat roof. Chickens clucked and scratched around the small backyard, along with several lambs. A grapevine provided both shade from the surprisingly hot sun and grapes that we would pick and eat whenever we wanted.

My family in Palestine was sprawling. On my mother's side was my grandmother Sitty Sarah, Grandpa Atif, aunts, uncles, and countless cousins of all different ages. A shepherd, Grandpa Atif was a wonderful human being, a caring and gentle man whom I loved very much. He was always excited to see us. My father's side was led by Sitty Halimah. Yaba's father, Grandpa Ahmed, had passed away just a few years before. Like many Palestinian women, my grandmothers and aunts all worked from home, raising their families, though some women ran home-based businesses. Between the two sides, I had eight uncles and one aunt.

My grandparents were particularly proud of my siblings and me because, even though we lived in the United States, we were able to speak and write Arabic. As I grew older, I would even read the newspaper in Arabic.

My siblings, cousins, and I would ride horses into the hills with other children from the community and help Seedy Atif mind his sheep and pick fruit from his orchards, under Palestine's crystal-blue skies. In this land where both Jesus and the prophet Muhammad had once walked, I could feel the history and spirituality in the air. Though most people drove cars or walked to get around, it wasn't uncommon to see people on horseback or even riding a donkey. I felt like I'd gone back to a bygone era.

On Friday evenings beginning at nine we would attend sahra, a party held the night before the weddings that would take place every weekend. Each evening the breeze would cool the air just enough that we would need a sweater. On weekends the adults would sit under the shade of the beautiful olive trees, eat, drink tea, and talk. Olive trees are very symbolic in Mediterranean cultures, where they've provided medicine, food, a source of livelihood, and more for thousands of years. Generations of the same family have unfolded under these trees, as they've cared for the plants, picked and enjoyed their succulent olives, pressed olive oil, run businesses based on the trees' wood or their fruit, and lived in harmony.

Living aromatherapy

Another aspect of life that was different from Brooklyn was that the air in El Bireh was always fragrant with food. The aroma of freshly baked bread wafts through the air, as do the smells of lemon and berry trees.

Even going grocery shopping was a sensory experience. Vendors proudly stacked fruits and vegetables high in pyramids under the big open-air tent in the community's shopping district. Bright red pomegranates, peppers, and tomatoes; green apples and emerald cucumbers and parsley; orange carrots and clementines; sunny lemons—the market was a riot of color and fragrance. And there were tons and tons of grapes. Red grapes, green grapes—grapes everywhere, perfectly colored and round, just like somebody had painted them. Crunchy and sweet!

Typically I would go to the market with my grandmother Sitty Sarah. The market is a very lively place full of vendors engaging with customers, yelling to one another, and playing Arabic hip-hop and traditional folk music from the boom boxes they place under their tables.

"Good morning, Hajja?" one of the businessmen might say.

"Good morning," Sitty Sarah would respond, picking up and inspecting the tomatoes. Sitty Sarah would always wrinkle her nose. "Ten shekels for three kilos of tomatoes?"

Unlike in American stores, where the price is already set, shopping in Palestine requires negotiation.

"Yes, Hajja," the vendor would reply. "Freshly picked, firm and succulent. Go ahead, taste one! You've never had better."

"Everyone sells tomatoes," my grandmother would exclaim, putting four kilos of tomatoes into her basket and handing him four shekels.

"How can I live with such low prices?" the man would ask.

My grandmother would smirk and walk off. The men might have deep voices and talk loudly, but the women would usually get their way.

I loved to pass by the men standing in front of metal barrels of hot oil, frying falafel, a delicious ball or patty made of smashed chickpeas flavored with onion, garlic, parsley, coriander, cumin, black and cayenne pepper, and other ingredients. The vendors would lovingly place each patty into a piece of freshly made bread, smoosh it, and give it to me for about a dollar.

But in Palestine if you can't go to the market, then the market would come to you. Individual vendors can come to your house straight from their farm, bringing fresh watermelons, or figs so sweet that it's like they are filled with honey; very different from the figs you get in the United States.

"The fruits and vegetables are so fragrant and flavorful because the land and soil are holy," Yumma would tell me. "There is spirituality everywhere, even in the vegetables."

I loved to sit in the backyard, where the sweet smells of cucumbers, lemons, and grapes lingered in the air. It was like living aromatherapy.

CHAPTER 6

Curfews, Raids, and Checkpoints

The ground in my grandparents' backyard suddenly started to rumble.

My cousins stood still in horror, with their mouths gaping open, faces blanched.

"This is a curfew!" a man's voice crackled ominously over a loudspeaker from the direction of the street. "Everybody back inside."

My cousins raced frantically across the yard to the back door. Even the chickens clucked and the sheep froze. One time, one of the sheep went numb and literally toppled over.

The first time we heard the man over the loudspeaker, my siblings and I just stood there with our faces scrunched up. *Who are these men, saying that we have to go inside and stay inside? What do they mean? It's not nighttime.* None of it made sense.

Suddenly Yumma appeared at the door.

"Get in the house," she yelled at us, looking horrified. "Hurry up!"

We didn't understand, but we ran to the door and landed in her loving arms.

Before long I would associate the rumbling earth with the monstrous khaki-green or desert-tan Israeli army tanks that would slowly roll through the streets. Military snipers wearing olive-and-sand-colored camouflage and helmets, and carrying machine guns, would patrol the roofs of certain buildings. They could commandeer the top of any structure, even your own house.

Once the army placed El Bireh under curfew, no one could go outside. You couldn't visit your family, go to work, or open your business, or even go to the grocery store.

You never knew how long the restrictions might last—a few hours, a couple of days, sometimes weeks.

"Why are you so scared of the soldiers?" we'd ask. Or, "Why are we staying inside?"

When we were young, our elders would say, "Just do what you're told so we can all be safe."

Sometimes the tanks would announce something even scarier.

"All men over the age of sixteen, come outside."

Slowly the men and older boys would leave their houses in various stages of dress, hands raised or behind their heads. Women and children would cry and yell out to their loved ones, not knowing what might happen. You couldn't help but think, would your father or other loved one get shot, or would they be taken away and never come back?

Our cousins told us stories of parents, brothers and sisters, cousins, aunts, uncles, grandparents, and friends whom the Israeli army had taken away. Sometimes the captives would be gone for days, sometimes for weeks; others would never return. People never knew where the soldiers took them. Sometimes the soldiers even took children. There was no court, no judge, no jury to stand in front of to argue one's innocence to.

This type of tragedy was even visited upon by my mother's younger brother, Khalo.

Fingers through bars

One day I went with Sitty Sarah, my mother, and Khalo's wife to visit my uncle in jail. The day started very early. My grandmother awakened before dawn to cook rolled grape leaves, sweets, and other favorite foods.

When we got into the car, I peppered my mother with questions.

"Why are we going to a prison? . . . Why is Khalo in jail?"

Yumma told me that my uncle, who was just twenty-four, had been married for three weeks when Israeli soldiers arrested him while he was walking home. The military claimed he and about fifty other young Palestinian men had been involved in a rebellion against the Jewish state.

Khalo explained that he'd simply been going home to his new wife.

But his pleas had fallen on unhearing ears.

He'd been forced to appear in front of a military tribunal, which had found him guilty and incarcerated him.

Nobody had told him how long he would be held.

The city passed by in a blur as Yumma spoke. Eventually we reached the edge of a desert. There we joined several other families for a bus ride to the prison along a desert highway.

Four hours later we reached a one-story prison made of gray concrete blocks set against a tan-and-gray gravelly hill. The scrubby sand stretched into the distance as far as my eyes could see.

I fell silent.

Several soldiers met the bus and walked us to the front door.

Inside, one dimly lit hall stretched the length of the building. Cells lined this corridor, their bars green, the paint chipped. Each cell held at least ten men dressed in T-shirts and jeans.

Family members stood in the hall in front of the bars, speaking with their loved ones. They passed through the bars toiletries and fresh clothes, food wrapped in foil and waxed paper, and books, magazines, and other reading material.

Finally we reached Khalo's cell, where we visited with him. I remember my uncle and his wife lacing their fingers through the iron bars and sharing a kiss before letting go.

Another year would pass before my uncle would be released from jail.

Contention

During the ride back home, my mother told me the recent history of my people.

For thousands of years everyone who'd lived in the region

had coexisted, whether Muslim, Christian, or Jew. Each of the three religions credit the same person as a key founder of their faith—a man named Abraham. Palestine was a spiritual place, a peaceful place, Yumma said. A place where both Jesus and the prophet Muhammad had walked. She told me that lots of people traveled to Palestine to connect with their spirituality, to connect with God, connect with Jesus, connect with Muhammad. Unfortunately, that's part of what has made it such a contentious place. The struggle, I learned, goes back hundreds of years, but after World War II some particularly difficult events took place.

An international organization called the United Nations decided that Jewish people from Europe, many of whom had experienced the horrors and tragedies of the Holocaust, needed a safe place to live. The UN planned to turn part of Palestine into a new nation, Israel.

Israel would be the homeland for Jewish people. But there was one big problem: Palestinians had lived on that land for centuries.

Nevertheless, on May 14, 1948, more than half of Palestine was given to Israel.[3]

The next day, May 15, hundreds of thousands of Palestinians fled the area,[4] and by 1949, about as many people who currently live in Seattle or Denver or Washington, DC, had had to abandon their homes and their property.

The historic city of Jerusalem—which had been in Palestine since before Jesus—was split. Arabs, including Palestinians, were segregated into East Jerusalem; only Jewish people could live in West Jerusalem.

It didn't matter how many generations had occupied their property; Palestinians were displaced very aggressively. Tanks knocked down family homes and flattened mosques; possessions were taken, pastures were commandeered, and cemeteries and olive groves were ruined. More than four hundred villages were destroyed.

Hundreds of thousands of Palestinians were driven off their land with no place to live. Many amassed on the West Bank of the Jordan River, where they and their descendants still live today. Others fled into neighboring Jordan, Syria, Lebanon, and Egypt. These refugees were prohibited from returning home.

None were compensated for their loss.

Ever since, May 15 has been known as Nakba Day. "Nakba" is the Arabic word for "catastrophe."

These events caused great suffering in my family. As a result of losing their land, some of my relatives became refugees overnight. Today there are approximately seven million Palestinian refugees worldwide. Seventy-four years after half of Palestine was given to Israel, the refugees remain displaced. Within Israel and Palestine, the majority of Palestinians are restricted to territories occupied and controlled by Israeli security forces. The wrong that was committed has never been righted. I have cousins who now live in a mukhayyam—a refugee camp—where they share a square one-room cinder-block house on the outskirts of town, in a ravine down below a sidewalk.

Among the realities that make the situation so complicated is the fact that approximately 140,000 European Jewish

Holocaust survivors traveled—also as refugees—to live in this new country, Israel.[5]

No justice, no peace

Of course, if someone took your land, you would do everything in your power to get it back. So, ever since their displacement, Palestinians and other people of Arab descent have been fighting back against this injustice and the countless other injustices that followed and continue to take place.

This is called intifada—the uprising against the Israeli Occupation of places where Palestinians have historically lived.

"I was sixteen when the Jordanian army tried to draft me to help protect the West Bank," Yaba once told me. My father was born four months after Nakba Day in 1948, so it's no wonder my grandparents named him Nidal.

Yaba believed in the cause but had no interest in being a soldier. A very loving and peaceful young man, Yaba moved to Kuwait to live with an older brother, before deciding to return home, in 1966, at the age of eighteen. The journey back to El Bireh took him through Amman, the capital of Jordan. Little did he know that eighteen was the exact age when men in Jordan were being conscripted into the military. Suddenly Yaba, who had left home to avoid entering the military, found himself drafted, stationed in Kuwait, and unable to return home.

One year later, in June 1967, various Arab nations stood up against Israel in what became known as the Six-Day War. That week Israel seized a place called the Gaza Strip from

Egypt and the West Bank from Jordan. Suddenly, movement between Jordan and the West Bank was restricted and people needed permission and papers in order to travel. Ever since, people have had to pass through military checkpoints, protected with barbed wire and crawling with soldiers, even to travel from village to village.

Eventually Yaba returned to Amman. Several years later he ran into his brother Nabeel, who had married and had been living in Amman. Nabeel told Yaba that their other brother Mohammad had married and moved to New York. Yaba knew that he must find his way to America, the country he had been taught was "the land of the free." So he applied for papers to join Mohammad.

Generation to generation

I am told that Seedy Atif began suffering from depression after he lost his land during the Six-Day War. When my parents, siblings, and I would come to visit, he would stay inside a lot. But every now and then he would go outside and doze under the azure sky.

One day I couldn't find him in his usual places.

"Where is Seedy Atif?" I asked. Since nobody seemed to know, I went looking around the neighborhood.

"He's sitting over there by the gate," one of my cousins told me, pointing toward a lawn chair in front of the barbed-wire fence that surrounded the village.

The image of him sitting in front of the razor fence was jarring.

"Grandpa, why are you sitting here looking at the barbed wire?" I asked as I sidled up beside him.

My grandfather took a deep breath, paused, and then responded.

"See those beautiful trees?" he asked, pointing toward some olive trees in the distance.

"Yes, Seedy."

"Those are my trees," he said. "But I can't get to them anymore."

"What do you mean?"

"They were my trees, and my father's trees before that, and my grandfather's trees before that, and my great-grandfather's trees even before that," he said. "These trees have been passed down from generation to generation."

"Why can't you get to them?"

"Well, you see this barbed wire? And you see this gate all around us?"

"Yes . . ."

He then shared how Israeli settlers had taken over the land and then built a barbed-wire cage around it, electric on top, so no Palestinians could enter.

"This is our life under Occupation," he said.

Learning what the Occupation had done to my grandfather, cousins, uncles, and other loved ones was very eye opening and transformative.

While the lambs, donkeys, and horses in Palestine that we didn't have back in the US were novel and fun, I became much more aware of things that other kids like me seemed not to be looking at. Over the years I would both witness and hear about armed Israeli soldiers pulling people's sons out of their homes and making them lie in the street, take off their clothes, and cover their eyes, as the soldiers searched them. I thought of the times when Palestinian kids would get taken away—"disappeared," people called it—for a week or two at a time. I considered how my Sitty Sarah must have felt when my uncle Khalo had first gotten arrested and when she and Grandpa Atif had gone looking for him. When they hadn't been able to find him. When there's no number to call. When a loved one has simply gone missing.

I began to think deeply about the people my parents descend from and are connected to.

Five minutes from my cousins who live in the refugee camp, Palestinians who had returned to El Bireh after becoming prosperous overseas had built extravagant mansions. The contrast of my cousins' poverty in the shadows of such tremendous wealth felt very wrong to me.

After learning so much about my people's struggle, my family's trips to Palestine never felt the same. My innocence and sense of being carefree were gone.

Now that I knew the story of my people, resistance bubbled in my blood.

CHAPTER 7

New School, New Rules

Finally the time had come to make the big step of going to high school.

High school was a huge deal in my family. My father's formal education had ended in the fifth grade. My mother's future had been bright academically, but she, too, had left school—when she was sixteen. So having their children get a high school diploma became my parents' educational American dream.

It didn't matter if it was at public or Islamic school, I was always the first kid to class, and I sat in the front row. I took pride in learning and would read everything we were assigned and ask the teacher for more. I was always on the honor roll and at the top of my class.

But in New York getting a good education can be a big struggle. There are specialized high schools that focus on academics, but you have to apply to get into them; some parents start preparing for this when their kids are in kindergarten.

I wanted to attend Midwood High School at Brooklyn College, in a neighborhood called Flatbush, about five miles away from my home. Midwood had a gifted and talented program. My neighborhood school, John Jay, did not. In any case, there was no telling if you'd get in. So I put together a list of my top picks and presented it to my mother.

"Midwood?" Yumma frowned. "Never heard of it."

"It's near Flatbush Avenue?" I said, trying to help her feel comfortable, since the school was near a well-traveled commercial corridor. Even though I was a teenager now, my mother still paid close attention to where I went.

"Flatbush?" Yumma repeated doubtfully.

"Abdo is going to go there," I said of the oldest child of our Yemeni next-door neighbors.

"Hmm . . ."

Yumma rummaged through a dresser drawer and pulled out a dog-eared subway map, then laid it out on the bed-spread, smoothing its wrinkles with her palms. She carefully counted the number of train stops between our house and the school.

"You will have to switch trains."

"Yes, Yumma, it's just on the other side of the platform." I fidgeted nervously while she studied the map.

"Too far," she announced.

"I could take the subway with Abdo."

"Where is Rosa going to school?" she asked of another neighbor my same age.

"John Jay," I mumbled, the disappointment rising about

the prospect of attending my neighborhood high school.

"You can ride to school on the train with Rosa."

As far as Yumma was concerned, I could learn at any school as long as I stayed out of trouble and applied myself.

John Jay was one of our nation's founding fathers. In 1789, President George Washington appointed Jay to be the first member of the US Supreme Court. About six years later Justice Jay ran and was elected as the second governor of New York State. I imagine that at some point the school named after him had provided students with a good education. But by the time I arrived, it was securely parked upon the city's worst-schools list. The school system had turned it into a dumping ground where schools from all over Brooklyn sent kids who were seen as having discipline problems, who were on the verge of dropping out, or, like me, who hadn't been admitted to one of the city's highly competitive magnet schools.[6]

"Dang, girl, why you going *there*? You know they call that place Jungle Jay, right?" Abdo said when I told him where I was going. We were sitting on the concrete ledge that separated our houses, watching our little sisters play hopscotch on the sidewalk. John Jay was rumored to have a lot of gang activity. To hear the grapevine tell it, the Crips, the Bloods, the Latin Kings, the Papi Chulos, and others were recruiting there. He frowned as he said, "I'm telling you, Linda, watch your back."

I tried to play it off, but after spending the summer hearing my friends tell me how tough the kids at John Jay were, I'll be honest—I was nervous.

This is not right

I remember my first day at John Jay like it was yesterday. Yaba drove me to school in our Chevy Suburban.

Who rides in such a ridiculous car? I wondered about the hulking and conspicuous burgundy beast I normally loved.

When we stopped at a light about two blocks away, I could see a stream of students, almost all Black or Latinx, walking from every direction toward the hulking redbrick building. Nobody's father was driving them to the door on the first day of ninth grade.

"Hey, Yaba, I'll just get out here," I said, then quickly grabbed my book bag, pushed open the door, and jumped down to the sidewalk just as the traffic signal turned green.

"But, Linda . . ."

"See you later, Yaba!"

I slung my book bag over my shoulder and darted across the street as he yelled after me in Arabic. I raised a hand in acknowledgment, though I hadn't heard what he said.

Dodged that bullet!

I fell in with the stream of students walking toward the campus, feeling jittery but eager to meet up with Rosa, who had taken the train and was going to meet me inside the front door.

Some of the older students hoisted themselves onto the sidewalk railing, talking and laughing. A tall, skinny girl with waist-length locs high-fived a girl with a short 'fro. Another girl joined them, her mane of shiny black hair catching the morning sun as she squinted like she was looking for someone.

I walked past a police car parked along the curb. Two

officers sipped coffee, ate bagels, and surveyed the arriving students. As far as I knew, there was a squad car stationed outside every high school.

Rosa was standing inside, as we'd planned, looking fly in her black jeans, red Converse high-tops, and cropped denim vest.

"'Sup, girl," I said, bouncing up, full of nervous energy. "You ready for this?"

She didn't answer.

Her arms were folded tightly across her chest, and she was watching several long lines of students preparing to file through large metal detectors like the ones you see at the airport.

"Put your bag on the belt and walk through the scanner," several adults shouted. "Put your bag on the belt and walk through the scanner."

Without missing a step, kids laid their purses, book bags, and fanny packs on the X-ray belt. The metal detector beeped, pocket change jingled into metal bowls, and book bags zipped and unzipped.

"Hey, girl!"

"Yo, what's up!"

Kids' voices echoed as they greeted one another, but Rosa and I inched forward through the checkpoint.

On the other side, adult monitors lined kids up against the wall and waved security wands from the students' feet to their shoulders, focusing on their book bags.

"Turn around," the monitor would command as they moved their wand around the young person's body. Occasionally one would start beeping.

"Open your mouth," the monitor would say, before sending the kid to a side table for further inspection.

"Unzip your bag," the student would be told. Or, "Turn your pockets inside out."

"Why I gotta open my bag? Dang!" some brave soul would occasionally protest. I would worry whenever a kid spoke out. I knew what could happen back in Palestine to people who pushed back.

"Do you really want to be sent home on the first day of school?" a large, matronly-looking woman asked, gesturing toward a Latina-looking girl's topknot. "Take down your hair," she said matter-of-factly. The security monitor ran plastic-gloved fingers through the girl's hair. Finding nothing, she gestured for the girl to move on.

Next up was a Black girl with long micro braids. "I just styled it, Miss . . ."

"That's not my problem."

The monitor grabbed and squeezed the young woman's hair by the handful. The girl rolled her eyes and stared at the peeling gray paint on the wall, as though she were used to this treatment.

What is happening here? I wondered.

I touched my own hair, which I'd pulled back from my face in a half ponytail. I hoped I wouldn't get sent to that table too.

Justice or just us?

The high school named after Chief Justice John Jay had a law-and-justice theme and offered an educational track to teach students about the criminal justice system, and prepared them for careers in law enforcement.

The school had its own model courtroom, with a raised wooden dais, defendant's and plaintiff's tables, a witness stand that faced the courtroom, and a jury box where jurors would listen to the lawyers plea their cases. In the back of the room, chairs were lined up like in a legal gallery, where an audience could sit and watch.

But in reality the school felt a lot less like it emphasized justice and more like it emphasized prison. The energy in the air reminded me of the Occupation.

All the windows had padlocked iron screens or vertical bars. Police officers stood outside and regularly stopped and frisked students. There were police officers on every single floor and at every single entrance of the school, with the innocent-sounding title "school safety officer." There were more cops in the school than guidance counselors. With only three guidance counselors for every four thousand students, the ratio was so bad that kids struggled to figure out how to get an appointment.

Ironically, even with all this so-called security, I often felt afraid.

What do they know that I don't know? I'd think every time I saw the police. Just their presence made me feel like something bad was going to happen.

But never once did I ever feel bullied or fear any of my classmates, 90 percent of whom were Black or Latinx. (There was a cluster of Asian kids, a few white kids, and maybe ten or fifteen Arab kids in the entire school.)

As an adult I would learn that John Jay had been what we call "over-policed," where even common teenage behaviors such as eye-rolling, talking back, resisting rules, and fighting were met with the heavy hand of suspension, expulsion, or even being charged with a crime. Most schools with lots of students of color—as well as the communities they live in—are over-policed, a reality that doesn't exist in predominately white communities. In hindsight I realize that the fact that the school was organized around law and justice was unconscionable, hypocritical, and ridiculous.

Empire State of mind

Not many students at John Jay were Muslim, but no one treated me differently or even seemed to care that I practiced Islam. But on the flip side, no one understood my faith, so sometimes I felt a little alone.

Because of this I'd insist on going to school during the Eid holidays.

"Whatever holiday plans you've got, we'll do them after three o'clock," I'd tell my parents.

My mother hated the fact that my studies meant more to me than a religious holiday, but I wanted to have perfect attendance.

The fact that my family was from Palestine gave me cool points with a handful of kids. Although most seemed not to know about the military occupation of Palestine, a few knew that Palestinians were oppressed.

A whole new group of hip-hop artists was rapping about our struggles. That made me feel proud. Method Man had a rhyme "P.L.O. Style."

"Oh what a tangled web we weave / When first we practice to deceive."

Still, most kids had the same response Jalal had had when I told them my family was from Palestine.

If you're Black in America, you visibly belong to a particular group. Granted, being Black in this country comes with great risk, but you can claim your culture with pride, and no one questions who you are.

With my dark straight hair and very fair skin, I didn't look the way many people stereotypically believe most Middle Easterners look. Plus, my name, Linda, means "pretty" in Spanish, and I had a heavy Brooklyn accent that made me sound a lot like the actress Rosie Perez. Lots of people just assumed I was Puerto Rican. Or, since Sunset Park sits next door to Bay Ridge, where a lot of people of Italian descent live, others figured that I was Italian. Being seen as racially ambiguous, I felt almost invisible. And when I tried to be proudly Palestinian, people's confusion bothered me. I was always adding more explanations. Always trying to prove my national and cultural origins. Always trying to establish my identity.

Sometimes I'd wish my parents had named me "Fatima" or something else that would have caused people to see me as Arab, or at least Muslim. In those early years I longed for a way to showcase my identity as a Palestinian American Muslim young woman.

CHAPTER 8

Finding My Voice

I really loved school, aside from feeling frustrated that people didn't understand my identity. Reading especially was something I enjoyed. It allowed me to mentally travel beyond my surroundings. I particularly liked *The Autobiography of Malcolm X*, about a young African American man who experienced a spiritual conversion from Christianity to Islam. I also read all kinds of poetry and loved Emily Dickinson. One particular quote that stood out was:

> *I know nothing in the world that has as much power as a word. Sometimes I write one, and I look at it, until it begins to shine.*

Poetry became my way to express myself. I would pen poems about growing up Palestinian in Brooklyn; about my immigrant parents, their experiences, and their sacrifices; and about my father working long hours. I also wrote a lot about my school. I became a wonderful writer.

I got this!

It was in math class that I found my first mentor.

Mr. Rodney Harris, who was also our assistant principal, was known for taking groups of students under his wing. In a school where many of the teachers just seemed to be putting in their time, Mr. Harris was different. Tall and African American, he stood out in a school full of mostly white women teachers. Not only did he wear a suit, tie, matching handkerchief, and cuff links each day, but he also arrived at school with a high sense of purpose. Mr. Harris never sat in his office—instead he was always moving around. The cafeteria. Gym. Hallways. He mentored the new immigrant kids, the gay kids, the Black kids, the kids who had been in trouble with the law. He saw our potential, and expected us to live up to it.

Even after my math class ended, Mr. Harris never stopped checking on me.

Rosa and I became part of a group of girls he met with regularly, along with our friends Samantha, Cecily, and Kenisha.

"Hey, ladies, let me see your report cards," he would say.

If our grades weren't where he thought they should be, he'd pepper us with questions to get at why we might be having trouble, and offer suggestions for how we could do better. If he didn't think our courses were challenging enough, he'd encourage us to change classes.

"You really should get involved," he would say about extracurricular activities.

"Why should I get involved in the drama club? I'm not going to be an actress!" I would ask.

"This isn't about what you'll do for the rest of your life. It's about learning what's fun and what's not, and what you like and don't like," he would tell me. "The more extracurricular activities you engage in now, the more chances you have to explore aspects of life that you may not even be thinking about."

"But I have to be home from school at three fifteen."

"Well, tell your mom what you want to do and ask her if you can come home a little later."

"I'm sure she won't let me."

"Well, have you explained why it's important?"

"No . . ."

"Okay, this is what you tell her," he'd say, and help me strategize about how to convince Yumma.

Truth be told, at first it wasn't really about my mom. I didn't understand how fun extracurricular activities could be, or how they would help me connect with things that I love.

"Okay, let's sign up for drama club and debate team," I suggested to a couple of friends, partially because we were curious and partly to get Mr. Harris off my back.

Turns out, drama club was wonderful. I loved reading different plays and acting out different parts. But it was being on the debate team that really surprised me.

Even when I was challenged to take a side of an issue that I didn't agree with, I was good at finding ways to research and defend my positions.

My friends and I practiced our debating skills and eventually began to prepare for our first mock trial, where you role-play and imitate what happens in a real court.

"In a mock trial you have to deliver opening and closing statements," our debate teacher told us. "So you have to prepare your statements in advance."

Though most of the other kids would get butterflies in their stomach, I had a natural talent for speaking up and not feeling afraid. In fact, the mock trial felt like a very natural place for me.

"Let me see your closing statement," the debate teacher said to me.

"Don't worry, I got this," I told her, certain I could walk out there without writing out a formal statement like the other kids did.

"Where is it?" she asked.

"Right here," I said, handing her a piece of notebook paper.

"This is incomplete."

"How is it incomplete?"

Being on the debate team had made me confident enough to debate her about whether I was prepared.

"This is just a list of points," she answered. "From looking at it, I don't understand what you're saying."

"That's because you haven't seen me deliver my closing statement yet."

"I need you to write out all your points first."

"Let me deliver my closing statement, and you let me know if you think it's incomplete," I responded. I'd already learned that I'm not a person who can read off a paper. Other kids may need to write it all out, but that's just not who I am. "You cannot determine whether or not I'm prepared based on what you see on my paper."

"Okay, Linda," she said to me. "I'll trust you this time, but you'd better prepare."

On debate day I nailed my closing statement. Paper or not, I said what I needed to say. I looked at her with a smirk, and she looked back in a way that said, *Darn it!*

In debate I excelled. I developed the skills to stand up for myself and my ideas. Before long I became one of the best debaters in the school. Debate made me stronger in drama club, and drama made me feel more confident when I debated. I could think on my feet, make good decisions in the moment, and stand out when I was in front of people.

Activities outside the classroom can change your life and broaden your horizons. If you haven't already, I encourage you to try them, whether at school; at a mosque, temple, church, or religious center; in a sports league; or at an after-school program at the Y or Police Athletic League.

But I had no idea how important those skills would be in helping me fulfill my life's dreams.

CHAPTER 9

Over-Policing

"Fight! Fight! Fight!" the kids yelled as they leaped from their seats and circled the two boys wrestling on the cafeteria floor.

Rosa yanked me back from the action that had suddenly sprung up around us.

"What's going on?" I asked, surprised that Ricardo, this really quiet, short, tan-skinned kid with a short-short haircut was now grappling with Mateo. With a little earring in his ear and his signature jean jacket, Ricardo was a bit of a pretty boy. He had been left back a year and didn't really mess with anyone. He also didn't have the same lunch period as me, so when I'd seen him striding purposefully in our direction, I'd known that something was up.

"I heard Ricardo's pissed 'cause Mateo's been talking to his girl," Rosa told me, helping me catch my balance as I slipped a bit on the chocolate milk and mac-and-cheese spilled on the lunchroom floor. "I'm staying outta that mess."

Mateo was an older, bigger, and much taller Dominican kid who wore the oversized, really baggy jeans that were popular back then. He was eating lunch just a couple of seats away when Ricardo crumpled up a piece of paper and launched it at his head.

At first the guys cursed, threw food, and pushed each other back and forth. At some point one shoved hard enough that several food trays clattered to the ground and they both ended up writhing on the floor.

Two lunch monitors pushed through the crowd. "Break it up. Break it up!" they yelled as they pulled the boys apart.

That's when we heard a big commotion at the door.

Several police officers came storming in.

"EVERYBODY BACK!" they screamed as they charged across the cafeteria.

Kids screamed, ran, climbed over furniture, and tried to hide in the corner. Chairs flew, tables were knocked over.

"GET ON THE GROUND! GET ON THE GROUND!"

Why are the cops here? And why are their guns drawn? Why are they telling kids already on the ground to get on the ground?

"No, please don't!" the two boys cried as they each curled into the fetal position.

"LIE ON YOUR STOMACH!" one cop yelled at the top of his lungs.

Both boys froze.

"LIE ON YOUR STOMACH!"

Whoa! Is this normal?

"What did I tell you? *GET DOWN ON YOUR STOMACH!*"

Both boys rolled over, pleading, "Please, no! My mother . . ."

The cops humiliated and handcuffed Ricardo and Mateo, then led them away as one cried, "My mom is at work. Please don't call my mother."

All the kids stood there, stunned. Ricardo and Mateo were just about the most un-scary boys in our entire school. Everyone knew that the police response had been chaotic and unnecessary. Some of the teachers looked shocked. Even they knew that it really hadn't been that serious.

Later we heard through the grapevine that the cops had taken Ricardo and Mateo to Central Booking and charged them. We didn't see them for several days. I'm uncertain whether they were in custody or had been suspended from school. All I know is that two of the least scary people in the whole school now had police records, and all because of a fight over a girl. That was not okay.

I wanted to inspire

I wouldn't learn until I was much older that this sort of thing wasn't happening at high-performing high schools like Midwood, or predominately white or suburban schools. Instead this type of excessive discipline, force, and policing overwhelmingly takes place at schools whose students are predominantly Black, Latinx, and or Indigenous. However, even within predominately white schools, Black and Brown students often get disciplined for behaviors that teachers tend to overlook among white kids.

For all my life up to that point, I had trusted the police, but the more I discussed the situation with my Black and Brown classmates, I learned that most feared the police and had experienced injustice at the hands of the cops.

"Once, I saw my uncle get beaten by the police," one classmate told me.

"Yo, once the cops dragged my uncle out of the house," another shared.

No wonder my classmates were so panicked. I hadn't seen my family members being stopped and frisked, handcuffed, abused, or even beaten by the police, so I hadn't looked at cops as a potential enemy.

Or had I seen my family members treated that way?

Back in Palestine my relatives experienced the random force, excessive punishment, the injustice, and the occupying authorities.

I began to wonder what the teachers had been thinking. Who had called the cops in the first place—and why? What had made them think that was appropriate to do? Why hadn't any of the teachers told the cops to chill out? Afterward, did any adult stand up to say that the situation was wrong?

Judging by how shocked some of the teachers had looked, perhaps they too had felt powerless to intervene, or perhaps even to say we shouldn't have cops in our school—much less with guns. Guidance counselors could have handled this and much of the other garden-variety teenage misbehavior better, but with so few of them, police officers regularly trooped into our midst.

As the cops continued to occupy John Jay, it became clear that I had a lot more in common with my Black and Brown classmates than I'd initially thought. Later I would discover that my father had embraced this truth for years.

When I was fifteen I watched the movie *Dangerous Minds*, starring Michelle Pfeiffer. In a nutshell the film is about this "bad school" with a lot of students of color from difficult backgrounds—perhaps they were poor, one of their parents was incarcerated, or a parent was dead, something like that. Actress Michelle Pfeiffer plays a high school English teacher who loves and believes in the kids.

The school in *Dangerous Minds* is a lot like John Jay—full of wonderful students dealing with situations far more challenging than mine. I saw the kids in my school. And I already understood the impact that someone like Mr. Harris could make, because of the impact he'd made on me. Now, watching the role Michelle Pfeiffer played, I dreamed I would return to John Jay and inspire kids through literature, reading, writing poetry, and telling their stories.

I knew that they had so much to share with the world. So being a high school English teacher became my dream.

CHAPTER 10

My American Dream

My education was the pathway to my aspirations.

Unexpectedly, one morning during my junior year, my guidance counselor stuck her head into my homeroom.

"Linda, I need you to come to my office."

Oh, shoot. What now?

I followed her down to her office, feeling anxious. She pulled out my transcript.

"Just so you know, that's it," she said.

"What do you mean?"

"You have met every requirement," she told me. "You've taken all your classes, you've passed all the exams, and you've completed all your credits. You could graduate."

"Graduate?"

"Yeah, graduate."

"When?"

"Right now," she said.

"That's not what I want to do, though," I said. "I want to graduate with my class."

"Why would you want to stick around and hang out in high school for another year? It makes no sense to stay and do nothing."

So just like that, high school was over.

"Get a cap and gown," she said.

I graduated at the end of eleventh grade. No final debate for debate club; no senior-class play; no participating in the fashion show with my peers. No college counseling; no help filling out a college application; no looking forward to spring semester of senior year; no class trip; and definitely no prom. My parents had this crazy idea that all the kids that went to prom did really bad things.

I cried as I said goodbye to my classmates. I knew I would probably never see many of them again. But as disappointed as I felt about how high school ended, my graduation was a huge triumph for the Sarsour family. I, Linda, had successfully achieved my parents' American dream. That was a family triumph—and we had all made it happen together.

Three months later I enrolled as a first-year student at Kingsborough Community College, located at the opposite end of Brooklyn in a community called Sheepshead Bay.

I was the second person in my extended family to attend college, and the first girl. At this point I was embarking upon my own American dream.

I couldn't forget

Now seventeen, I had also reached the age at which Palestinian girls were considered old enough to think about marriage. In fact, that summer a number of girls I knew got married.

At one wedding in Brooklyn, I saw a young man wearing a white long-sleeved shirt, black slacks, and a black tie, with his hand shoved deep into his pants pocket. He looked familiar. I realized he looked a lot like Sitty Halimah's next-door neighbor Maher, from El Bireh. Could it really be him?

"Hey, I know you," I told him.

Maher seemed taken aback that I'd approached him. In Palestine it would be very uncommon for a Muslim woman to start talking to a man she barely knew. But this was America. My friends and I could talk to whomever we wanted without our parents criticizing us.

"I know you too," he replied with a quick smile.

"I didn't expect to see you here," I replied, wanting him to feel comfortable so far from home.

"The groom and I grew up together," he explained. "I came for the wedding. I'm staying in Boston."

Our interaction was brief, but his smile flashed brightly in my imagination.

A week later his father reached out to my father to ask if Maher could call me.

Yaba agreed.

"Most Americans can't pronounce my name, so everyone just calls me Mike," he said.

"In Crown Heights everyone calls my dad Nick," I replied. "But his given name is Nidal. It's really not that complicated."

We compared notes about how different my upbringing in Brooklyn had been from his in El Bireh. It was nice having so many common references. The fact that my parents had raised me with a strong connection to Palestinian culture allowed our conversation to flow freely, and it helped that I was fluent in the local colloquial Arab dialect. Two hours later the first conversation I'd ever had with a young man came to a close.

We continued to talk. In time he came to Brooklyn to visit me. Later I would learn that Sitty Halimah loved him like a son and secretly hoped he would marry me. To her delight, he eventually did.

Seeing myself

A riot of turquoise, scarlet, sunshine, and violet spilled onto the carpet of my parents' living room.

"Pick out whatever you want," one of my mother's best friends, Um Sharif, offered after lugging her overstuffed suitcase up the front steps and into the house.

"Lena, Heeba, Hanady, and Hela—come look," Yumma called.

It was a chilly Saturday morning in April 1999. Um Sharif had just returned from Mecca, Saudi Arabia—Islam's holiest city. She'd just completed hajj, the five- or six-day spiritual pilgrimage that Islam asks all Muslims to take at least once in their lifetimes if they are able. Afterward, many shop. Some of the world's most exquisite abayas and modest dresses can be found there.

Yumma, my sisters, and I crowded around, oohing and aahing as we sorted through the beautifully sewn abayas, luxuriously woven scarves, velvety sticks of black kohl, and assorted hijabs.

"Ooooh, Heeba, that would look so good on you," Um Sharif cooed encouragingly as my fifteen-year-old sister held a long, ocean-blue abaya with gauzy sleeves against her jeans and faded yellow T-shirt. Heeba struck a pose in front of the full-length hall mirror as Yumma stood at her shoulder, one hand tracing the brightly colored embroidery that adorned the sleeve.

"Just beautiful," our mother agreed.

Quietly I picked up a black two-piece hijab and slipped it over my dark, shoulder-length hair. No one noticed as I walked toward the mirror.

"What do you think?" I asked them.

The voices around me hushed one by one. My mother and Heeba stepped aside so I could see myself. A young unmistakably Muslim woman stared back at me, her chin high and her kohl-lined eyes alive. It was the first time I'd ever worn a hijab.

By this point Maher and I were married. I was even pregnant with our first child. When I looked at myself with the hajib on, I felt something inexplicable stir within me.

A knowing.

Gently Yumma adjusted the soft black cloth, then touched my cheek. "It suits you, habibti," she whispered, honoring the moment's unexpected reverence and sensing, along with my sisters, the emotion welling up in my chest. Gazing into the gilt-edged mirror, I felt as if I were seeing my true self for the first time.

This is it.

Short and small, those three words held a lifetime of searching for my identity. I now had a way of showing who I am that gave me a clearly visible identity in the world. Finally I appeared to the world exactly how I felt on the inside: generous, courageous, humble, compassionate.

Unapologetically Muslim.

CHAPTER 11

9/11

The September morning dawned clear, crisp, and crystal-line blue. The campus of Kingsborough Community College looked particularly idyllic, with its expansive emerald-green lawns and vistas overlooking the boats bobbing in Jamaica Bay.

I sat in my nine a.m. chemistry class taking notes. Our professor, an older white man, was extremely straight-faced and strict—no beepers, no pagers, no cell phones (not that many of us had one back then).

"No electronics in the classroom," he'd tell us.

So, many of us started giggling when his cell phone started going off in his suit's breast pocket. Looking surprised, he reached into his pocket and squeezed the phone silent. When it started ringing again, he pulled the phone out, looked at it, and walked out of the classroom without even saying "I'll be right back."

We chatted and waited. Fifteen minutes later he still hadn't returned. That was odd, but since that was the time we were required to wait if a teacher ran late to class, we packed up our notebooks and started leaving. As we left the classroom, our teacher was nowhere to be found. Everyone walking around looked kind of stressed, so I figured that something bad might have happened on campus.

I headed toward the building's entrance, pushed open the door, and walked into all these little snowflakes coming down. I held out my hand to see what they were. Burned pieces of paper. Something had clearly happened.

"Yo, what's going on?" I asked the security guard.

"All I know is that a plane crashed into the World Trade Center," he answered.

"What do you mean?" I asked, figuring that maybe a flock of geese had flown into one of the plane's engines, causing it to fail and the pilot to lose control. Hadn't something like that happened in the nineties? Or maybe a small propeller plane had hit the building. Maybe it had been a news team reporting on the weather.

"I don't know," he said. "They're saying it's really bad. A building fell down."

That's when it dawned on me that maybe the wind had blown the paper pinwheeling around me all the way from Manhattan, more than ten miles away.

A chill traveled up my spine.

The end of the world

My first instinct was to get to Sunset Park, where my mother was babysitting my two children, Tamir and Sabreen. I waited almost an hour for the bus before someone told me that New York City's entire mass transit system had been shut down. I had no option other than to walk the seven miles home.

"A terrorist attack . . . ," I overheard someone say as I trudged westward.

Oh God, I hope it's not Arabs. Please let it not be Arabs.

By the time I reached Bay Ridge, it was early afternoon. The place was a ghost town. All the shops were shuttered, and mosque doors were bolted and padlocked. A deep hush had fallen over the neighborhood. I stared at the smoke rising in the distance and covered my nose and mouth from the stench. My stomach queasy, I didn't want to think about what might be unfolding across the river. I wasn't ready yet to know about whatever had been so disastrous that it had silenced Brooklyn's streets and the rumble of trains underground.

The moment I knocked on my mother's front door, she came running out of the house, car keys in hand.

"I have to get DJ," she cried. My eleven-year-old brother was part of an honors program across town.

"Yumma, your hijab . . . ," I called out as she entered her car. "You aren't wearing it."

"Linda, we can't today," she called back. "It's too dangerous."

My stomach somersaulted as she coaxed the car's engine to life and sped off. Inside, Sabreen was dozing peacefully in her baby bouncer. I stooped alongside Tamir, tousling his spiky black hair.

"Fire, Mommy," he said, his little hand pointing to the television screen. "Look, Mommy, fire. Fire. Fire."

He kept repeating the word in a kind of daze.

And that's when I saw it—not one but both of the twin towers engulfed in flames. Then the massive structures knelt almost operatically, crumbling one after the other to rock and dust, dense plumes of ash billowing around them. The images sucked the breath out of me. For days a continuous video loop was shown of buildings buckling and papers taking flight like frantic doves. Beneath the horrific images scrolled the words MUSLIM HIJACKERS ATTACK WORLD TRADE CENTER.

That was the end of the world as I knew it.

A moment of clarity

It was September 11, 2001. Over the coming days we would learn that in New York City alone 2,763 people had died, including more than four hundred first responders. One hundred eighty-nine people were killed as a plane hit the Pentagon right outside Washington, DC. A third plane filled with forty-four people went down in a Pennsylvania field as several passengers fought with the hijackers on that plane. Almost three thousand people were killed in all, including the nineteen hijackers. The people who died came from seventy-eight countries.[7]

The extremist organization al-Qaeda claimed credit for the deadliest attack on American soil in US history. The nation and world were shocked and horrified.

At one point my friend Rifah asked me to walk with her

to visit her cousin a few blocks away. We strapped our children into their double strollers, hoping that the short journey would distract us from our grief. On the way we ran into Um Ahmad, an elderly Palestinian woman. She was sitting on her stoop, one hand shading her eyes from sunlight as she studied the faces of dead heroes in a newspaper spread across her lap.

"Assalamu alaikum, cheef halich?" I greeted her, asking in a Palestinian dialect how she was doing. I bent and kissed her three times on the cheek, feeling the softness of her wrinkled face. Well into her eighties, Um Ahmad circled my neck with her thin arms. Then she patted the concrete step next to her.

"Listen to me," she said as we sat beside her. Her ancient eyes peered deep into my soul, and she gestured toward our head coverings. "This is not the time to wear your hijab in the streets. Faith is in the heart, and God will understand. Right now he wants you to be safe."

By then the nineteen hijackers had been identified, and most had common Muslim names—Mohamed, Saeed, Ahmed, Khalid—names the same as our own kin. But these men were not our family.

"Um Ahmad, those terrorists have nothing to do with us," I protested. "A lot of Muslims died in the attacks too." It was true—sixty Muslims had perished in the towers alongside their coworkers.[8]

"I know," she said, shaking her head sadly. Rifah and I were naïve, but Um Ahmad already saw what might be coming. As a young woman in Palestine during the war of 1948, she had lived through the nakba, and now she feared that another sort of catastrophe had been set in motion. "But the news is making it about us. Those hijackers shared our faith."

I knew she was right, but I wasn't convinced that I should stop wearing my hijab.

"The hijackers may have been Muslim, but theirs was not the faith we practice," I said. "Islam is an expression of peace."

"Young people, listen to me," she begged.

As my thoughts reeled, I flashed back to the messages I'd received at Islamic school—about compassion, about generosity, about community, about love.

These were all values to be proud of and lean into.

I recalled times when my parents had insisted that we speak only Arabic at home. I was particularly grateful to be fully bilingual and proud. If ever there was a time to represent the good in Islam, to oppose the evil those men had unleashed on our world, this was it.

I'm Muslim, I thought. *This is who I am. Why should I hide myself in shame?*

I would not take off my hijab, I resolved.

Automatic suspects

In the ensuing days, family members frantically roamed the streets of New York City, plastering the walls of buildings, construction sites, subways, and shop windows with the faces of their missing loved ones, and asked pedestrians whether they had seen these people who had disappeared. The faces of dead firefighters, medics, cops, and people who had worked at the World Trade Center stared out from the newspaper in row upon row of photographs. I studied their faces for hours.

Many people began branding Muslims as terrorists at a dizzying speed. Others confused Islam with terrorism as though the two were synonymous. Then through its National Security Entry-Exit Registration System, the US government policy targeted Muslims in ways that proved our leaders believed Muslims were risks to America's national security,[9] a policy of great bigotry and intolerance.

I began to feel conspicuous in my beloved Brooklyn. When my mother and I walked into our supermarket wearing our hijabs, we could feel the air shift as some of the very same people who on September 10 would have smiled or said hello now held us in their gaze for a beat too long, as though we were suspects, before looking away uncomfortably.

And then strange things started happening. Suddenly husbands, fathers, uncles, brothers, and sons stopped returning home.

They hadn't made it to work.

They hadn't stopped by the newsstand.

They hadn't passed through the hookah shop.

They hadn't attended the mosque.

No one had seen them in days.

What is happening? I wondered.

Then came the rumors of Muslim men being picked up on the street. Speculation began circulating that the government was taking them. At first these stories seemed too different from what we'd been told about America to be true. Yet we heard more and more very disturbing reports.

"They flashed their badges and told us he had to come," one woman at the mosque recounted about her husband, her eyes wild with terror. "What were we to do?"

"Did you ask who it was or where they were taking him?" another would ask.

"They wouldn't tell us."

"My brother never came home from work," a different woman sobbed, her body folded over. "I don't know where he is or what I should do."

Day by day the number of missing men grew.

"Please help me, Imam," family members would beg.

"I will try, but no one is returning our calls," our imams would tell them. "We don't know what to do. The government is surveilling us, too!"

Unmarked cars parked outside our mosques. Plainclothes agents watched as the faithful came and went. Then paranoia began sweeping through our communities as people feared government spies and informants were in our midst. If someone, even a friend, asked your opinion of recent events, you wondered if the question was innocent.

In Arab-owned shops and hookah lounges, television sets that previously had been tuned to the mainstream television networks were tuned only to sports channels, or even turned off entirely. Shopkeepers dared not air news programs that could provoke political conversations.

In a matter of weeks we had all been transformed from ordinary, everyday New Yorkers who happened to be Muslim into automatic suspects of a heinous terrorist act.

The Danger of a Single Story

In 2009 a storyteller named Chimamanda Ngozi Adichie gave a speech about the danger of a single story and stereotypes. You can watch it online.

A stereotype goes something like, "All _____ people are _____." When we stereotype a group of people, we automatically assume things about them based on one story we've heard. Most of the time these things aren't true about every single person in that group—or perhaps even most people in the group.

For example a lot of people have only heard one story about Islam. Unfortunately, this is the story of 9/11. Because the men who committed the violent acts on 9/11 called themselves Muslims, some people think that all Muslims are violent. Of course, this is not true. Still, many people treat Muslims poorly because of this stereotype.

It's important to remember that the actions of only a few people don't represent an entire group. Be curious and learn other stories and perspectives. Don't let one story you hear become the only story you know.

CHAPTER 12

Basemah

Maybe three Fridays after 9/11 happened, several women who lived in the same building in Bay Ridge came into the mosque begging, "Help us, help us!"

"These men came to our house and they took my husband," one cried to the circle of women that formed around them.

"They took my son," another sobbed.

At the time the other women at the mosque were all immigrants; some barely spoke English.

"What do you mean somebody came to your house?" I asked, feeling thankful that I spoke both English and Arabic, so I could understand everyone present and everyone present could understand me. "You can't just take someone and not even allow him a phone call."

I took the women to the imam's office. Originally from Egypt, he too was an immigrant. He didn't know the law or his rights, and English wasn't his first language. Horrified and helpless, he turned to me, and we began calling immigration attorneys. Suddenly I found myself visiting people whose loved ones were missing and getting vital information from them—their loved one's date of birth, alien number (the unique number the federal government assigns to every non-citizen who lives in the United States[10]), and so on—as well as working with the immigration lawyers who were trying to find the missing family members.

My fabulous older cousin Basemah was experiencing something similar. In the years since my childhood, she had gotten divorced, found an apartment, obtained a job at a hospital, and as a single mom raised her son—things that, culturally, women in our community just didn't do. Some people gossiped about her for violating some traditional norms, but Basemah didn't care what other people thought. Realizing that no social services existed for Arab women who had fallen on hard times or were facing the types of challenges she had overcome, a few months earlier she had founded an agency, the Arab American Association of New York.

Word traveled like wildfire. Basemah did not judge people; she did not make them feel ashamed, or spill secrets. Women trusted her with the most intimate details of their lives, so they came to her for help.

It was December when Basemah reached out to me.

"We need organizers and translators," she told me. "We need your skills."

Immediately I felt compelled to help. Also, you didn't say no to Basemah Atweh. So later that day I climbed the narrow flight of stairs to the AAANY's offices, which were located on the second floor of the offices of Dr. Ahmad Jaber, the obstetrician who had delivered my siblings and me and was known among Brooklyn's Palestinians for his generosity.

"I'm so happy you're here, habibti," Basemah greeted me. The room was full of women, many in hijabs. They sat in folding chairs at long white Formica tables. Some were in distress and were being advised or comforted. Basemah wanted me to help people find their loved ones and obtain services to take care of their family.

This is America

"Tante," said a little boy, tugging on my tunic and calling me "auntie" in French. I squatted down so I was level with his face. "Tante, will you find my baba?"

The four-year-old had big brown, earnest eyes framed by long, thick eyelashes. He reminded me of my own son—the dark eyes, shiny black hair, and absolute innocence and trust.

"Yes," I told him. "We're going to find your father."

It was the very first case I worked on. I recall it like it was yesterday.

The boy's father had disappeared into the abyss of law enforcement agencies. He was Moroccan, and he had come to the US three years earlier, approved by the US government to work here. As the manager of a company that imported goods, he had been responsible for setting up an office in the New York City area. One evening as he sat down to dinner with his wife and son, someone knocked at his door. When he opened it, three white men in civilian clothing stood in the hallway.

"May we come in?" one of the men asked. Assuming they were law enforcement, the Moroccan man stepped aside and let them enter. In many Arab countries if the police stand at your door, you let them in and follow their instructions, unlike in the United States, where you could ask if they had a search warrant and might refuse to speak to them without having an attorney present. The men went through the family's belongings and documents.

"Please come with us," they told the man when they had finished. The man didn't know where they were taking him, or why, but felt he had no choice but to obey. After four days passed with no word from her husband, the wife was distraught. The imam at her mosque suggested she contact us.

"Who were these men?" I asked in Arabic. "Where did they say they were from?"

"I don't know," the woman responded, wringing her hands.

"Call the legal clinic at Brooklyn Law School," one of the other women volunteers told me, sliding a phone book across the table. "Tell them your name and what you know."

I called, and a friendly-sounding voice picked up on the other end.

"Hello, my name is Linda Sarsour," I began, feeling uncertain. "I work for the Arab American Association of New York."

"Oh, yes, hi!" the person said.

"I'm calling about a Moroccan man who some authorities

took from his home," I explained. "He's been gone for four days now, and his family doesn't know where he is."

"What is his name?" the woman asked.

And just like that, my career as a human rights advocate and community organizer began.

Each day I worked with legal clinics to try to figure out where this child's father might have been taken. Eight days later we finally located him in a federal high-security prison where, among other things, the government jails people who have been charged with committing federal crimes that the government believes could be particularly dangerous. Because he had traveled extensively for his job, his passport contained stamps from many Muslim countries. For some reason, having those stamps in his passport had made our government fear him. Their further investigations had found nothing remotely suspicious, so when our lawyer petitioned, they released him.

The next day I was sitting at the table doing paperwork when I felt arms being thrown around my waist.

"Thank you, tante," the kindergartner with the big eyes said to me. I looked up and saw his mother and a man I assumed to be his dad. She hugged and thanked me and handed me a box of baklava.

"We are so grateful," said the man, reaching out to shake my hand. "If you had not come looking for me, I would have been deported."

"Your wife is the reason we found you," I told him, placing a hand on his little boy's head. "And your son, too."

My eyes filled with tears as I watched this reunited family

leave our office that afternoon, the man with one arm around his wife and the other around his son. I thought about my own children, realizing that the America in which my son and daughter would grow up was now a much less hospitable place than it had been during the joyful era in which I had been raised. Exhaustion and tremendous sadness overtook me. At the same time I felt a strange kind of exhilaration. I had delivered on my promise to a little Moroccan boy, and that felt profoundly meaningful to me.

Because I spoke both Arabic and English, I had attended a law-and-justice high school, and I felt confident in using my voice, people began to ask for my help. And word travels fast in our community. After I was able to help a woman find her husband, she told somebody. That woman then told somebody else. Women would find out whose daughter I was and show up at Yaba's bodega asking for me.

"Sister . . ."

And I'd help.

In time we discovered that often men would be held at a detention center either in downtown Manhattan or in Elizabeth, New Jersey. I began to go there with families. Sometimes I would stay with the woman's children in the car while she visited her husband. As a new mother who had young children of her own, I could feel the injustice in these moments. Other times I'd go inside, where the strong stench of urine would singe my nostrils.

This is not okay.

Yet I began seeing how everything I'd experienced in my life thus far—being of Palestinian descent, speaking fluent

Arabic, loving to learn, attending a criminal-justice high school, learning how to stand up for myself to make an argument, choosing to wear a hijab, even being a young mom—had prepared me for this moment. Perhaps I wasn't supposed to be a high school English teacher after all. I was rising to fulfill what seemed to be an even greater need. These were my neighbors. They were people of my culture. They spoke the same language, ate the same foods, went to the same park. All I wanted to do now was help them, knowing that their very survival might depend upon my efforts.

God had brought me new opportunities to contribute to humanity, make myself useful, and serve. I understood my place perfectly. I would use my voice. I would stand up for vulnerable people. I would fight for what is right. In the shadow of unimaginable tragedy, and the fear and suspicion of Muslims that had followed in its wake, a new flame burned inside me.

CHAPTER 13

The Accident

Steve Jobs, the founder of Apple. *Today* **show host Hoda Koth.** Actors Salma Hayek and Vince Vaughn. Entertainers Shakira and DJ Khaled. These are among the many Americans who people may not know are of Arab descent. I could go on and on.

The public celebrated Americans of Arab heritage on May 5, 2005, at the new Arab American National Museum in Dearborn, Michigan, outside Detroit, home to one of the nation's most concentrated Arab American communities.

To get there Basemah and I drove ten hours in Dr. Jaber's dark green 1994 Toyota Avalon, along with Angie—Basemah's cousin—and Mona, a twenty-five-year-old Palestinian AAANY volunteer. Dr. Jaber and his wife drove themselves separately.

Attending the museum's opening ceremony was a big deal. Though Arabs have been present in America since its beginning, the Arab American museum was the first out of the thirty-five thousand museums in the United States to tell our story and commemorate our accomplishments. Nothing could have kept us away from this joyful occasion. The very existence of an Arab American national museum and its association with the Smithsonian in Washington, DC, felt like a triumph for our community.

My chest swelled as I stood on Michigan Avenue in front of the gray granite-and-glass building. I felt goose bumps when hundreds of people cheered as officials cut the opening ribbon.

I walked through the doorway with the rest of the crowd, admiring its azure-blue-and-gold mosaic.

"Look, Basemah!" I exclaimed, feeling awestruck by the lobby that soared for two stories overhead.

"Oh, sorry, sister," a woman said as she bumped into me. Everyone was looking upward.

"This is who we are. I feel so proud," Basemah exclaimed as she admired the beautiful Arabic scrollwork that adorned the building's dome.

Basemah, Angie, Mona, and I wandered through the jam-packed exhibit rooms, the sounds of laughter and excitement echoing through the grand halls.

Everything in this museum disproved the negative stories about Arab Americans that so many people had latched on to after 9/11. This museum didn't see us as dangerous extremists. Instead it celebrated our excellence and honored our accomplishments as American citizens. Finally the nation could see our true story.

At the end of the evening, Dr. Jaber and his wife left to

return to Brooklyn. Basemah, Angie, Mona, and I celebrated late into the night, planning to drive back early the following morning.

Make everything right

"I'm not going to lie to you, my eyes were closing before we stopped," Angie exclaimed the following morning. "I think someone else should take over."

It was only seven forty-five a.m., but as we walked back to the car with cups of coffee in hand, Angie held up the car keys. It had been four hours since we had left Detroit.

Basemah and Mona didn't drive, so the only "someone else" who could take over was me. I had my license, but being from Brooklyn, I hadn't driven a lot.

Yet as Angie held out the keys to me, it crossed my mind that she was my mother's age. If my mother told me she was too tired to drive, I'd simply take the car keys and get behind the wheel. Basemah sat in the front seat beside me.

I pulled out into traffic on I-80 and began cruising along, all of us chatting about the previous day. Before long everyone else dozed off, and I was alone with the mountainous terrain, countless trees, and my thoughts.

Somewhere in rural Pennsylvania, I started seeing signs announcing roadwork ahead. As the traffic narrowed from four lanes to two, I slowed down, keeping one eye on the tractor-trailer trundling along in the lane to my left. To my right was a steep drop-off into a grassy ditch, and no metal barrier to protect us from it.

To be honest with you, I felt nervous.

As my hands gripped the steering wheel, all my senses heightened. Soon a long row of orange-and-white traffic barrels came into view, marking off a construction area. Up ahead a barrel had fallen over and was lying in the path of the truck beside me.

That truck is big enough just to roll right over it, I thought.

Suddenly the driver veered into my lane. Panicked, I swerved to the right to avoid him. Instantly we were flipping over and bouncing down the steep slope. The car turned three full revolutions before landing upright, wedged in a muddy ditch. I seemed to be uninjured, but the passenger seat was empty.

Where is Basemah?

I heard a moan from the back seat and turned to see Angie grimacing in pain, her leg jammed between the front seats, bent at frightening angles. Mona too had disappeared. In that moment I realized that I'd been the only one wearing a seat belt. All of the doors were closed, but crushed and twisted, and all the windows had shattered.

I struggled to open my door. Once I did, I could see Mona, maybe forty feet away in the ditch.

"Angie, I have to find Basemah," I said. "I see Mona but I lost Basemah. I don't know where she went."

"Go, go." Angie waved me on as a new surge of pain contorted her face.

I ran to Mona, who was lying on her back staring at the sky.

"You okay?" I asked. She was clearly not okay.

"I don't know if I can move my back," she whispered.

Then she asked me the strangest thing. "Am I still wearing my hijab?"

"Yes, you are," I told her, pulling the cloth forward to cover her escaping wisps of hair. At least she was alive. I still had to find Basemah.

I ran back to the car, circled it, and found Basemah lying faceup on the far side of the car. There wasn't a mark on her. Her lips were moving, but I couldn't hear what she was saying over the roar of traffic above. I fell to my knees beside her and bent close.

"I can't breathe," she whispered. "Can't . . . breathe . . ."

"Hold on, Basemah! I'm going to get help."

I clambered back up to the road and began waving my arms, trying to flag someone down.

A blue pickup truck pulled over, and a young white man and his girlfriend got out.

"What's going on?" he asked.

I pointed down into the ditch, and he took out his cell phone and called for help. His girlfriend ran back to the pickup and emerged with a red-and-black plaid woolen blanket that she wrapped around my shoulders. I hugged the covering around me gratefully, but then I thought about how cold Basemah must be. So I slid down the slope and spread the blanket over her. She smiled weakly, her lips moving soundlessly. She was trying to tell me something.

"Shhh, it's okay," I told her. "Preserve your strength. The ambulance is on its way."

Everything seemed to be happening in slow motion, yet I don't think five minutes passed between the time when our car flipped and the moment when I heard sirens blaring and the *thump, thump, thump* of a helicopter overhead. Two helicopters landed. Police cars with flashing lights blocked off Interstate 80; ambulances and fire trucks screeched to a halt at the top of the embankment; paramedics carrying stretchers and first aid equipment raced down the slope.

I could tell from their urgency that Basemah was the most seriously injured. EMTs cut open her shirt and shocked her heart with electric paddles attached to a defibrillator.

"I can't breathe," she gasped over and over.

At least she's talking.

Firefighters sawed off the top of the Avalon to free Angie, as medics lifted Mona onto a stretcher and loaded her into one of the helicopters.

They shifted Basemah onto a stretcher as well and started an IV drip in her arm. Then they rushed her toward the second helicopter.

Okay, they have her, I thought. *They'll fix her and make everything right.*

It never once occurred to me that this could turn out any other way.

Shattered

The helicopters lifted into the sky with a loud roar, their rotors whipping up a whirlwind of grass and dirt around me. As I turned my face to protect my eyes, I saw Angie lying on a stretcher in an ambulance up on the road. A medic took my arm and led me up the embankment and into the ambulance with her. Once I was seated inside, the medic jumped into the back, pulled the doors shut, and signaled for his partner in the driver's seat to go. The siren came on, and we began to weave through the traffic.

Angie and I ended up at the same hospital emergency room as Mona, where we learned that several bones in Mona's back were shattered. Angie had fared slightly better. Her right leg was broken in three places. Basemah had been taken to a trauma center, so we didn't yet know her fate.

As for me, I thought I hadn't been injured at all. But hours later I looked down at my left hand and noticed it was covered in dried rivulets of blood. A piece of glass was embedded in my wrist. I had become a walking public service announcement for the importance of wearing seat belts.

But by being so physically unhurt, I felt incredibly guilty. Three women were suffering horrifically because of me. I sat in the hospital hallway, staring into space. I didn't know what to do but stay close to my friends.

After a while a young medical resident found me there, or maybe some kind soul sent him to me. He told me that he too was Palestinian American. He was generous enough to take me to his home, where his wife encouraged me to clean myself up and eat something. I was a sight, my face streaked with dirt, hair flying everywhere, eyes wild with shock and fear. My hijab had been knocked off in the accident.

"Look," he told me, "I know you're going through a lot of trauma, but you have to get your head straight. Who do you need to call?"

I thought of Basemah's son, who still lived with her in

Brooklyn. And I thought of her eight brothers and sisters. But how could I call any of them to say what had happened without first knowing how Basemah was? Better to wait for news, I decided. I didn't answer.

After a while—I have no idea how long—the resident took me back to the hospital. He was with me in the lounge area later when a doctor, an older white gentleman with snow-white hair, walked up. His expression was so somber, my whole body tensed.

"Is your name Linda?"

I nodded.

"What is your relationship to Basemah Atweh?" he asked.

"She's my father's cousin and my mentor, and she's like my older sister," I said. "She's . . . she's . . . everything to me. She's my . . . Basemah. . . ."

My words trailed off as I saw the doctor's eyes well up.

"What happened?" I asked him, my voice tiny and scared. "Where is Basemah?"

As the doctor sat down next to me, suppressing a sigh, I pulled the plaid blanket tight around my shoulders. But it could not protect me from what came next.

"Basemah passed away," he told me. "We did everything we could to save her, but there was so much internal bleeding."

I looked at him, trying for all I was worth to unhear his words. I'd never again get to hear her laugh with her whole being like she was having an asthma attack.

In my head a single thought ricocheted like a scream.

Basemah is gone.

CHAPTER 14

The Aftermath

Sometimes things happen in life that are so terrible, all you can do is put one foot in front of the other. Sometimes there's nothing you can do to change what is.

There was nothing I could do to take the accident back.

I sat in a hospital lounge without my hijab, draped with the red-and-black plaid blanket. The seconds ticked by so incredibly slowly. I stared into space. I counted the tiles on the floor. I looked at the TV blaring on the wall, but I didn't hear a word anyone said. Though other people walked through the room, I was so out of it that they might as well have been ghosts.

The world as I knew it was over. Nothing about it would ever be the same.

I called my father first.

"Yaba, we had an accident."

"Are you okay?" he asked me frantically.

"Yaba, I'm fine. Nothing's wrong with me. I didn't break anything. Nothing happened to me."

And then I fell silent.

Because how do you say the words you know will break your father's heart?

"What about everyone else?" Yaba asked quietly.

I think, by my silence, he knew.

"Basemah is dead," I said.

I will never forget the strangled sound of my father's cry.

And in that moment I realized why I hadn't wanted to call anyone when the young resident had urged me to. I hadn't wanted to utter the words that would make the accident real.

Yaba asked for details, and I offered them. I could hear that my voice sounded thick and ragged. I felt very detached, like I was floating outside my body, observing myself as unimaginable tragedy took hold.

Sorrow and guilt enclosed me, but my eyes remained as dry as the Palestinian desert.

So broken

After Yaba hung up, he drove to come get Angie and me and bring us back to Brooklyn. Mona would have to stay in the hospital for two more weeks as doctors worked to stabilize her spine. She would wear a body brace for years and have multiple surgeries, but she would eventually heal.

My mother began making calls to let people know we had lost Basemah.

Dr. Jaber began making arrangements to fly her body back to Brooklyn for her janaza—Arabic for "funeral"—the following day. In most cases Muslims must be buried within twenty-four hours of their death. So the imam at Basemah's mosque prepared for her service as soon as he heard the news.

That night I lay down in my old bedroom at my parents' house, still grasping the plaid blanket, while Maher stayed in Bay Ridge with our kids. The ritual washing of the dead had already taken place, and Basemah's pristine, unblemished body had been wrapped in pure white cotton for the funeral service, which would begin in a matter of hours. I felt as though I were moving underwater. Everything was muted by my crushing remorse at having robbed the world of Basemah's bright light.

I still hadn't cried by the time the janaza took place. Inside the mosque that afternoon, I could barely process what was happening. More than three thousand people had come to pay their last respects to the family and honor Basemah— people of all different faiths, races, and nationalities. People from the hospital where she had worked; clients she had once served; local politicians and activists; imams, ministers, and rabbis. All of us were heartbroken that Basemah had been stolen away.

Family members and friends went out of their way to console and assure me that I was not to blame.

"It could have happened to anyone," they said.

"It was just bad luck that you happened to be the one driving. . . ."

"It's a blessing that you weren't killed in the accident too."

"We're so relieved that you survived."

But even as people hugged and attempted to comfort me, my thoughts were dark: *Why do I get to live? Basemah was a mother too. Her son might be grown, but why should he and his future children be cheated of her presence? Why should any of us?*

I didn't go to the cemetery after the service. I knew that watching Basemah's body being lowered into the ground and hearing the dirt thudding onto her casket would be too much.

"Please hold things together at home," I asked my husband. Our children were six, four, and two by now. I didn't want them to see their mother so destroyed. Even though I was grown, I needed my mother.

I went back to my parents' house, to my childhood bedroom. I climbed back under the plaid blanket that I had thrown over Basemah as she'd struggled for breath in a grassy ravine.

Was it only one day ago?

It seemed I had aged a whole lifetime since then. I felt like a different person entirely, so broken that I didn't even recognize myself.

"Basemah loved you, habibti," Yumma said as I lay in her arms. I craved my mother's soft hand stroking the hair back from my temples. "She would want you to forgive yourself and move on."

That night, and for many nights after, I slept clutching the plaid blanket from that kind stranger in the blue pickup.

The rough wool against my skin felt like the last link to my life's greatest teacher. I had no idea how I would go on without her. And yet I still had not cried.

For Basemah

On Monday morning I dressed myself and went into work. Though I now worked for Lutheran Medical Center, I was stationed at the Arab American Association of New York. Lutheran encouraged me to take as much time off as I needed. But sitting at home, constantly remembering Basemah lying in the grass, fighting for breath, was unbearable. Better to keep busy, keep pressing forward. So on Monday morning I climbed the seventeen steps to the AAANY's offices and pushed open the door.

Everyone gasped and then froze.

"What are you doing here?"

"It's too soon for you to come back."

"Habibti, please, you must go home!"

Then they crowded around, hugging me.

And that's when the full force of Basemah's death finally hit me. Never again would she move through these rooms, laughing, energizing, and taking care of us with such purpose and her buoyant spirit. My knees buckled and I began sobbing violently. Yet even as I lay in a ball on the floor of the agency that Basemah had built, weeping as if I would explode from missing her, a powerful wave of commitment arose. In those moments huddled on the floor, I vowed to carry on her huge legacy.

This is how I'll redeem myself.

Soon I sat with my fellow staffers and volunteers around the long, white-topped Formica table, and we began to make a plan for the months to come.

"We have to continue this work for Basemah," I said, "because this is all she ever wanted. She didn't dream of riches or fabulous trips around the world. Instead she dreamed of an organization that would serve women who were like her, and everyone else in our community who might need our help."

That morning I silently promised myself, God, and Basemah that the organization she'd built would live on after her.

For the rest of my life I would strive to make her proud.

Rising up

That fall Dr. Jaber and his board of directors voted to appoint me executive director of the agency.

"Basemah prepared you for exactly this," they told me.

"I'm not sure I'm ready for such an important responsibility," I replied.

"You're ready," they told me. "There is no one better suited to step into her shoes."

"But I'm only twenty-five," I protested, fearful that at my age I didn't know enough.

"She invested so much in you, Linda," they said. "She sent you to leadership trainings, taught you how to organize community events, introduced you to influential people, and steeped you in her belief that all our work was, first and foremost, about caring what happens to other people."

Even as I welcomed their vote of confidence, I knew that no one would ever be able to fill Basemah's red patent leather heels. But I would spend my life trying.

I experienced some hard days. But between what I'd witnessed in my parents' sacrifice to make our lives better, the challenges people faced back in Palestine, and the resilience of some of my John Jay classmates, had I not seen people push forward through difficulty? No human being is spared the challenges of life, and I was no exception, so I chose to struggle through.

Before the accident, when I'd been Basemah's right-hand woman, I'd passionately supported someone else's mission. After Basemah died, I developed a clearer sense of purpose, and her mission became my own.

I pray that nothing this devastating ever happens to you, but if it does, please do not give up. If there's one thing I can tell you, it's that things do get better. Put one foot in front of the other, ask for help, and take tiny steps even though things may not yet be all right. Step by step, moving forward helps you to heal and, in time, to make everything all right.

If you become so depressed that you worry that you may hurt yourself, or if you see a loved one in that situation, a caring and compassionate person is always available to talk. Call the National Suicide Prevention Lifeline, offering support twenty-four hours a day, seven days a week: 1-800-273-8255.

CHAPTER 15

Tamir's Story and Sabreen's Campaign

One day at a time I stepped into Basemah's shoes. Before long I began to feel more sure-footed and even began to find my stride. As I did so, I began to experience a profound healing as people shone their love and appreciation of Basemah onto me too. Slowly I put myself back together and moved forward into a new life.

There were things that I found both satisfying and troubling while running the organization. But one thing above all others really troubled me—how Islamophobia and religious bullying harms Muslim kids.

One day during the summer camp we offered, I walked up to my son, Tamir, and a group of young people who were having a conversation.

"Hey, guys, what's going on?" I asked.

"Hi, Sister Linda," the boys answered.

"How do you feel about starting your new school?" I asked

one of them who'd be starting middle school. I knew he'd be losing some friends and perhaps be feeling butterflies.

"Sister Linda," he said, looking down at his shoes, "what if people ask me if I'm a Muslim?"

"What do you mean?" I responded. "You tell them that you're Muslim."

"What if I tell them and they hurt me?" he asked, his soulful eyes looking up at me. "They stabbed that cabdriver. Would it be okay if I just didn't tell anyone I'm Muslim?"

The question took my breath away. Earlier that summer a white man had stabbed a Muslim cabdriver and injured him badly.

"Oh, honey," I said, hugging him. "You don't have to worry. Your parents and your teachers will protect you. You should always be proud of who you are."

Even as the words came out of my mouth, I wondered if I was telling him the right thing. I couldn't guarantee this boy's security out in the world; I couldn't even guarantee the safety of my own children.

A powerful motivator

Tamir has always been a tender soul. I will never forget how at four years old he defended a little girl from an elder's playful teasing. My son adored this little girl, the daughter of friends from our Palestinian community. At a family gathering he declared that when he grew up, he would marry her. Then one of his elder aunts poked fun at his devotion.

"But, Tamir, don't you see how her ears stick out from her head?" she said, her eyes twinkling with mischief.

I watched my son pull himself up to his full height and place his fists squarely against his sides. "God made her ears stick out that way, and so they are beautiful," he declared.

When he reached eighth grade, Tamir began applying to high schools. Among several requirements to get into his first pick, he had to share a paper he'd written, with his teacher's grade and comments on it. On the cab ride to the interview, I read the graded English paper he'd selected.

"My life is like a NASCAR race," his paper began. "My life's engine shuts down, and I have to go into the pit to fix it. A tire goes flat. We go into the pit to fix it. After all that, I always go the right way."

I loved that my child was using a metaphor from a sport he loved and writing about how resilient he was and able to bounce back from his struggles. I continued to read on. In his essay he described a day when his math teacher had asked the class to solve a difficult equation that she had written on the board. The first student who came up with the correct answer would get extra credit on the next test. Everyone the teacher called on got the answer wrong.

"Going once," the teacher said. "Going twice . . ."

Tamir raised his hand and answered correctly. I smiled as I read because I know that even when he knows the answer, Tamir is rarely the first to respond.

"Of course you know the answer," a white kid shouted from the other side of the room. "You Muslims are good at math because you need to know how to make bombs."

WHAT?

My heart plummeted and tears rushed to my eyes. As I sat beside my son, I tried not to show him how hard those words hit me. He was a normal thirteen-year-old kid, yet his classmate had seen him not as bright, loyal, and kindhearted but as a future bomb maker simply because of the family into which he'd been born.

I took a deep breath and continued to read.

"Sometimes my culture is portrayed as the evil culture, but we are probably the most down-to-earth people anybody could know. One way people have put me down is by only thinking of my people as 'terrorists.'"

By this point I could no longer help it. I cried.

At first, Tamir wrote, he didn't know how to react to his classmate's ugly comment, so he went into his pit stop to decide how to respond. He chose to respond by laughing, as if the boy had just been telling a joke. Chuckling diffused the tension and allowed Tamir to go on with his day. But he felt troubled when he reflected upon the comment later. Perhaps he should have confronted the kid and pointed out his Islamophobia, he thought. In hindsight he wished he'd told his classmates that Muslims are good people, that we believe in God, and that our faith is about love and peace, not bombs and violence.

I began bawling my eyes out right there in the cab. Through my tears I could see that his teacher had written in pink marker on the cover page: "I am sorry this happened to you. Tamir, you have tackled very significant issues here. I can feel your passion, and writing from the heart is the best way to go."

"Why didn't you come right home and tell me what happened?" I managed to ask my son between sobs. "I would have defended you. You didn't have to go through this alone."

"I knew you were busy helping families fighting deportation," he told me. "I didn't want to burden you because that's so much more important."

I was still dabbing my eyes as we climbed out of the cab and walked into his prospective school.

It turns out that I wasn't the only person whom Tamir's essay touched. It affected the woman who interviewed him as well. Tamir was admitted, and his NASCAR essay became a powerful motivator for me.

Restorative justice

So, you know me. Now that I did know about Tamir's experience, I wanted to teach him about restorative justice, an approach to righting a wrong that emphasizes bringing a victim and offender together to repair the harm, rather than just stigmatizing and punishing the wrongdoer.

"No, Mom, I don't want to snitch on the kid."

"I'm not going to go to the school and tell them to punish the kid," I said, assuming the young man had made the comment intended as a joke. He probably hadn't realized that he was saying something hurtful or harmful.

"Mom, it's not cool."

"I want him to have the chance to know who you are," I

said. "And even though I'm your mom, I want him to know that I'm not upset with him. Islamophobia oftentimes comes from a place of ignorance; it doesn't always come from a place of hate. We are not going to attack him or make him feel 'less than.'"

So after Tamir understood that I wasn't going to embarrass him, get the other kid in trouble, or show up like, "Listen here, you are not going to talk to my child like that," he agreed.

I called the teacher and asked her to share Tamir's essay with the young man. I told her I wanted to meet the young man and have a compassionate conversation with him. At first she was a little anxious about how it would go, but after she heard my intentions, she agreed. All four of us sat in the classroom.

"Son, tell him how you felt about it," I said to Tamir. "There's nothing to be ashamed of."

"I didn't really feel good when you said that," he told his classmate. "But it wasn't serious enough for me to embarrass you in front of the class, even though you'd tried to embarrass me."

The young man listened.

"Yo, Tamir," he said. "I didn't really mean it."

"It's all right."

"I'm sorry," he said. "That was really messed up, now that I think about it."

"It's all good," Tamir said. "We're cool."

Sometimes people misunderstand you because they don't have the right information, but it's very important not to let things slide. The kid could have been on a journey toward a more offensive place, but we caught him early in middle school to let him know that his behavior wasn't cool.

Today I watch Tamir have very substantive debates with people on social media. He has learned how to combat things in a confident way that also educates people and gives them information.

Pride and joy

"Why do you let people say these things?" my daughter Sabreen yelled as she came running into my bedroom.

"What do you mean?" I asked, sitting up in my bed. "What's going on?"

She shoved her cell phone up to my face.

"*Look!*"

I scrolled through the comments on my Instagram page. She was right; some were horrible. Even worse, a few of them even mentioned my children. As a high school student, Sabreen was too old for me to protect her from all the online harassment that I experience. There was nothing I could do except comfort her and let her know that I take every precaution to be safe and would help her be safe—and I would hire someone to scrub those hateful comments from the internet. That was about it. So that's what I did.

Sabreen attended the Urban Assembly School for Law and Justice. I remember visiting for parent-teacher night during Sabreen's sophomore year. Donald Trump was running for election and pushing this idea that the country didn't want any more refugees, particularly Muslims. However, as I walked around the school, every class door and bulletin board had a sign that read BLACK LIVES MATTER, REFUGEES WELCOME on it.

"Seeing these signs makes me proud to be here," I said to Sabreen's adviser. I appreciated that the school was allowing students to express their political beliefs and had such an accepting environment.

"Well, that was Sabreen," she replied. "She ran the campaign in the school and went around putting up the signs."

Without even mentioning it to me, in her own quiet way, my child had become an activist and organizer, professing these beautiful ideas in a public manner. I burst into tears. Today one of the many things I admire about my daughter is how she puts her money where her mouth is when she feels strongly about something.

Hostile environments

Between Islamophobia, my work with the AAANY, and the police killings of Black people such as Trayvon Martin, Eric Garner, and Michael Brown, my children were watching real life in America unfold, absorbing this knowledge and becoming worldly, exposed to so many things.

"We are not the only ones being discriminated against," I would tell them, explaining that Rosa Parks, Dr. Martin Luther King, and other historic figures they were learning about at school had experienced racism and people saying bad things about them and trying to harm them. "Black people have had this happen for centuries; it's not just us."

I wanted them to know what it means and looks like to stand up for yourself. These incidents with my children provided a beautiful picture of who my kids were becoming and how they were absorbing my values, and showed that they saw a purpose in what I was doing.

Similar to how a rock tossed into a pond can create waves that travel to the opposite side of the pond, events have a way of rippling across time. Though September 11 took place in 2001, two decades later Arab Americans and Muslim Americans continue to experience hostile environments. Rather than being valued, many Muslim children are vilified and made to feel as though they don't belong—even those born in the United States.

No human being should be treated poorly because of who they are, or have to choose between parts of themselves in order to be accepted—whether they practice Islam, are African American, are an immigrant, are LGBTQ+, speak a language other than English as their first language, possess any identity that isn't considered mainstream, or all of the above at the same time. No matter how you identify—Black or white; Christian, Jewish, or Buddhist—you can help create a climate that allows every person to feel safe and valued and proud. Caring for one another is part of our higher calling as human beings.

What's an Upstander?

When you see someone being bullied or treated unfairly, you have two options: you can be either a bystander or an upstander.

A bystander *stands by* and watches as someone is being bullied. They do not try to stop the bully. They do not offer help to the person being bullied.

An upstander *stands up* to a bully. They try to help. Here are a few simple but powerful ways that you can be an upstander:

• **Be a friend.** Show the person being bullied that they are not alone. Show the bully that you support the person they're targeting, and they'll be less likely to bully.

• **Speak up!** Let the bully know that what they're doing isn't okay. You can just tell them to stop or to leave the person alone. A few simple words could get the bully to back off.

• **Ask for help.** Bullying can go on for a long time and can get out of control. Don't be afraid to ask for help. Talk to a teacher, a school counselor, a parent, or another adult who can step in when things get bad.

Standing up to a bully can be scary, but it is important to do what's right. By being an upstander, you are making a huge difference in someone's life.

If you're being bullied or want to learn more about being an upstander, check out these websites:

National Suicide Prevention Lifeline
SuicidePreventionLifeline.org
1-800-273-8255

Pacer Center's Kids against Bullying
PacerKidsAgainstBullying.org

It Gets Better Project
ItGetsBetter.org

STOMP Out Bullying
StompOutBullying.org

Kids for Peace
KidsForPeaceGlobal.org

Stop Bullying
StopBullying.gov

The Bully Project
TheBullyProject.com

Cyberbully411
Cyberbully411.com

CHAPTER 16

Hurricane Sandy

On October 29, 2012, Hurricane Sandy pummeled the New York metropolitan area and the New Jersey shoreline.

My childhood house shuddered, rain pelted the windows, and wind whipped around the roof and howled as it sent debris somersaulting down the street. Unable to sleep because the wind and rain sounded so frightening, we watched, awestruck, as the tree limbs whipped back and forth and tree trunks swayed under the wind's force.

"Look how fortunate we are to be together," I reminded my children as we huddled in my parents' house.

Knowing the storm was coming, the night before I'd taken the bookshelf, TV, and china cabinet—everything located near a window—in our apartment and pushed them to the middle of the room. I feared the wind itself might blow out my windows, or the humungous tree outside might either break some window panes or, worse, fall on the house.

We lived in a low-lying area of Bay Ridge, but I thought our second-floor apartment would be spared from any flooding. Still, I packed my kids up and went to my parents' house, since it sat on such high ground. So did one of my sisters and her kids. We waited for the disaster to come. If anything went wrong, we knew it would be better if we were all together.

Whoa! Did you see that? a friend texted me sometime during the night.

No, what happened?

I'm not sure, but a fireball just flashed across Lower Manhattan.

My thoughts quickly flashed to September 11.

Whoa! I hope everyone's okay.

At daybreak newscasters began to report on the devastation. Throughout New York, water had risen over boardwalks and promenades, washed over highways, cascaded down subway steps, and flowed into subway tunnels. An electrical transformer on Fourteenth Street had exploded, creating the fire my friend had texted about, and the lower half of Manhattan had been plunged into darkness.

Video of one neighborhood in Queens showed orange licks of flame whipping through the darkness from house to house, setting one hundred homes on fire.

In Brooklyn we had been lucky.

Rally together

Even though the storm was still raging the next day, the phone calls started.

"Sister Linda, did you hear about Staten Island?"

"Just what's on the news," I answered, knowing that much of that community's shoreline is exposed to the Atlantic Ocean. "What's going on?"

"The storm hit at high tide and under a full moon," came the answer. "The wall of water that came in from the ocean was about fourteen feet high."

"Oh no!"

Over the coming days there were news reports of residents in beachside towns who watched their living rooms fill with water, and their dining tables, dishes, armchairs, and refrigerators start floating. The gales mowed down trees that knocked power lines over as they fell.

There were reports filled with images of devastated communities.

One photograph in particular stopped me cold—a plastic bin full of antique dolls, white lace garments soaked and dirtied, limbs broken and tossed together beside the chain-link fence of a house. Alongside the bin someone had slung sopping-wet jeans, dresses, shirts, towels, and bedsheets over the fence to dry.

The picture was of Staten Island's Midland Beach, where seven-foot walls of water had flowed through people's homes, washing much of their lives out to sea. Streets had turned into rivers, and the muddy brown water still hadn't receded. Many people had stacked their belongings—couches, mattresses, black garbage bags full of clothing, the contents of drawers—on porches and in sodden yards, hoping the day-after sun would dry and keep them from becoming moldy.

The place looked like I imagined a Middle East war zone might.

Sadly, the survivors were the fortunate ones. More people had died in Staten Island than in any other area in the region hit by the storm. In fact, twenty-four of the forty-four fatalities in New York City came from that borough alone, most concentrated in Midland Beach.[11]

A humanitarian crisis was unfolding in my own backyard, and I wasn't going to wait around for someone else to tell me what to do. People were desperate. It was time to see who I could rally together!

So I called a local politician, Nicole Malliotakis, who represented parts of Brooklyn and Staten Island. Nicole is of Greek and Cuban heritage and the daughter of immigrants. Though I was a progressive Democrat and she was a Republican, and eastern Staten Island was a conservative Republican enclave, we'd developed a good relationship, and human needs were more important than any differences we might have.

"What can the AAANY do to help?" I asked her.

"Midland Beach is still without electricity or gas," Nicole said. "People can't even cook. Can you order some pizzas and hand-deliver them to local residents?"

Of course, by now you know that AAANY sprang into gear.

Within the hour we had rounded up a dozen volunteers, seventy pizzas, and numerous other donations from some of the very generous Palestinian families who owned grocery stores in Brooklyn, whom Basemah had introduced me to.

She had taught me that all I had to do was pick up the phone and say, I need this or that, and those families and many other members of the community would demonstrate zakat. No matter whether its relief work in Haiti, or rebuilding a Jewish cemetery that antisemites have desecrated, or supporting rescue work in the south after a tornado, Muslims are often among the first to come through.

People can change

"Please stack the toothpaste, toothbrushes, soap, deodorant, detergent, and other everyday necessities on the table," I directed once we arrived in Midland Beach. "Anyone is welcome to take what they need."

From there our volunteers fanned out in teams of two, going door-to-door with a stack of pizzas. I walked with a young Black woman with pink-framed glasses and exuberant natural hair.

"Would you like a hot dinner?" we'd ask at each house.

"Oh my goodness, thank you so much," the residents would answer. "You're a godsend!"

We had one pie left after knocking on half a dozen doors. The next house was a taupe-colored two-story with white trim whose contents were piled up on the sidewalk. We pushed open the front gate, walked up a short flight of steps to the porch, and knocked.

No answer.

Pumps sucked water out of the basement, and a thick black hose emptied the muddy flow into the street.

I knocked again.

Nothing.

We were about to walk back down the steps when the door opened just a crack. A pale, pinched face peered out at us.

"What are you doing?" a woman asked with a brusque tone and a frown. From both the look on her face and the sound of her voice, I sensed that she was taken aback to find an African American woman with natural hair and a Muslim woman in a hijab standing at her door.

"Good afternoon," I greeted her. "We're in the neighborhood giving out hot pizzas to anyone who wants one. Would you like a pie?"

At my greeting, she opened the door wider and stepped onto the porch.

"I'm so sorry," she whispered. The woman was small, thin, and hunched over inside a man's chambray shirt, and her flat brown hair lay damp against her head. She seemed fragile.

Now I was the one confused. Perhaps she hadn't heard me or was one of the Russian immigrants who'd settled in this part of Staten Island and wasn't yet comfortable speaking English. I thought of my own mother when she'd first arrived in New York, and I spoke more slowly.

"We're volunteers and we're giving out free pizzas—"

The woman interrupted me, waving her hands in front of her face in a gesture that looked poignantly like surrender.

"I'm really sorry," she repeated, her words not seeming to connect with what I'd just said.

"Ma'am," I said kindly, wondering if perhaps she was

struggling with her mental health. "Would you like a hot pizza?"

"I didn't know," she said. "I just didn't know."

My partner looked as confused as I felt.

The woman pulled me by the sleeve to the edge of her porch and pointed to the back of her yard, beyond the water-logged trees stripped of their bark and leaves.

"They were going to build a mosque over there, right where the old Catholic church used to be," she said. "They were going to use the same building, and everyone said it was going to be bad, and that the people who were coming were dangerous."

As she paused and wiped her face against the sleeves of her shirt, I could see that she was quietly crying.

"I didn't know," she said, and explained that she'd marched against the mosque. "I just knew what they told me. They said it would be the same kind of people."

"What kind of people?" my partner asked, shooting me a glance.

"You know, the Muslims," the woman said.

She looked away from us, her eyes roving over her ruined belongings piled in the street. Then she looked up at the now cloudless blue sky.

"Terrorists," she said at last. "They said the terrorists hate us and we don't want them in the neighborhood."

She described how a Catholic priest had tried to convince the community to welcome the mosque. She had been part of the group that had picketed his front lawn. He'd also received death threats.

"And now you're here," she said. "I should have known better."

I thought of my son, and how he'd wished that he'd told his classmates, "Muslims are good people too." But this was hardly the moment to lecture this woman on why she didn't need to fear people who were only seeking to pray together.

"You know what?" I said. "Those people bought another building a few avenues over, and they're doing great. You don't need to worry about them."

"Oh good," she said so softly that I barely heard her.

"Besides, now you know better," I added. "People can change."

With that, we gave her the last pie and wished her a good recovery from the storm. She stood on her porch holding the pizza and watching us as we walked away.

That night I reflected that if I had not been wearing a hijab, the woman would not have known that it was a Muslim who had shown up at her door.

Now she did know that two women of color, one who worshipped as a Muslim, had knocked on her door and offered to feed her. I dared to hope that the next time she met a woman in a hijab, she would remember us and be somewhat less biased.

For a few brief minutes in hurricane-ravaged Midland Beach, we'd been just two women who had recognized each other's humanity, and had both walked away with hearts opened and hope renewed.

I like to imagine the impact rippling out across her world. If one person can change one other person's perspective, then that person might impact two other people—or more. They, in turn, could undulate out to five or ten people. This way one person can become infinite!

That's how we can come together to take on any problem and make the world a better place.

CHAPTER 17

Sajida's Voice

Not only was change rippling across the world, but it was also rippling across the dinner table and down the hall in my own home. Now my nine-year-old daughter, Sajida, started to get involved in what was becoming our entire family's collective stand for social justice.

For seven years the Coalition for Muslim School Holidays, a group of organizations in New York City, had been working to add Eid al-Adha and Eid al-Fitr to the calendar of school holidays. Christian and Jewish high holy days like Christmas, Easter, Rosh Hashanah, and Yom Kippur were already on the school calendar. The coalition, which I was a part of, believed that Islamic holidays should be honored too. Every year Muslim children were asked to choose between observing their spiritual traditions and receiving their formal education on that day. So the Coalition for Muslim School

Holidays tried to have Muslim high holy days added to the academic calendar as days the schools would close. That was when we had to figure out the solutions to a series of challenges.

The first challenge? New York City closed its schools on Christian and Jewish holidays because so many *teachers* observed these holidays that it cost less to close schools on those days than to hire substitutes. Since very few of the city's teachers were Muslim, we based our campaign on the number of public school *students* who identified as Muslim.

That was when we ran into our second challenge: city officials mistakenly believed that most Muslim children attended private Islamic schools that weren't under the city's control. But in reality 95 percent of Muslim children in New York City attended public school,[12] and one of every eight public school students was Muslim.[13]

Then came the third challenge. The dates of high holy days in Islam are based on both the lunar calendar and the location of the moon in the sky.[14] In fact, following an ancient Islamic tradition, many imams don't announce when the Eid holiday will fall until a few days beforehand, when someone in Saudi Arabia climbs on top of a building and looks at the relationship between the crescent moon, the sun, and the earth.[15]

"Our academic calendar is set a year in advance," one official told us. "We can't wait till the last minute to tell our teachers and students, 'Oh, don't come to school on Tuesday because it's an Eid holiday.' That's just not going to work."

Good point.

Creating allies

We hired an astronomer to calculate twenty years' worth of dates for Eid al-Adha and Eid al-Fitr, so that the Department of Education wouldn't have to figure that out.

But taking that step created an unexpected challenge. All over the world, Muslims set the dates for these holy days by looking at the moon in the sky. The idea of making astronomy calculations in advance defied tradition for some. Not everyone liked it. So various Islamic leaders and groups joined to talk about our differences and find a way to agree. American Sunni Muslims united with American Shia Muslims. African American Muslims aligned with Arab and South Asian Muslims. Palestinian Muslims came together with Pakistani Muslims and Muslims from Indonesia. All of us had in common that we wanted what was best for our children—and the fact that we'd been targeted by anti-Muslim policies and religious profiling by law enforcement made it easier to focus on our similarities.

For once we were not merely defending ourselves from being attacked or condemned. We were learning what we could accomplish when we all collaborated and worked together. The campaign united us in a way that we profoundly needed. And one of the most exciting aspects of the conversation was watching immigrant mothers become very involved and watching Muslim mothers lead the way.

But joining together among ourselves was just our first step. We would need to amass a legion of support by reaching out to other communities. So we thought long and hard about why adding Islamic holy days to the academic calendar was good for everyone, no matter their religious or ethnic background. Our campaign could be defined by three words: recognition, inclusion, and respect. We wanted young people to know, "You matter; your faith matters; you have a right to be who you are and to not apologize for it."

Next we reached out to leaders and groups representing other religions, races, ethnicities, and nationalities.

"We want an inclusive, respectful society for everyone, not just Muslims," we told them. "These principles are important no matter who you are."

We staged rallies, held community meetings, and wrote articles for the newspaper to answer questions, address people's fears and concerns, and attempt to win their support. Then we decided to ask people to sign petitions. Before long we had collected tens of thousands of names.

In a sense this campaign was our love letter to Muslim children.

Flipping the script

Unfortunately, not everyone agreed with us, so we experienced lots of setbacks and great disappointments. But sometimes life isn't actually telling you no; sometimes life is telling you *not now*. The challenge is just waiting until the time is right. Apparently the time wasn't right.

Yet.

So we waited.

One year turned into two years.

Two years turned into three years.

We kept biding our time, all the while building relationships with our friends and allies so that we would be stronger when that perfect moment arrived.

Finally the tide began to turn.

The time had come for New York City to elect a new mayor. We believed the mayor should represent the interests of all the city's residents, Muslims included.

So we decided to invite the candidates to the Islamic Center at New York University to speak to us. We invited every candidate and all our allies to attend. Members of New York's Muslim community were ready to demonstrate our clout.

We also invited a local imam to ask the candidates about the Muslim school holidays. We figured they'd take him seriously and give a stronger answer to the question. But the night before the forum, the imam called me.

"Sister Linda, I'm not going to be able to make it tomorrow," he said. "I'm sick and in bed. I'm so sorry."

"Brother, you just take care of yourself; we got this," I assured him. But I'm not gonna lie, my stomach turned a somersault.

"Who can we find at the last minute with the same degree of authority?" I asked some of the other leaders.

"What if a child asked the candidates the question?" one of them replied. "How could a candidate tell a child no?"

"Great idea," everyone agreed.

And what better child than Sajida, who had been part of the campaign all along.

Kid power

Sunlight streamed through the floor-to-ceiling windows of the New York University auditorium, where seven candidates now sat onstage.

People of every description filled the room's six hundred seats: Black, white, beige, Brown, Latinx, Arab, Eastern European, South Asian, young, old, mixed-race, gay, straight, trans, cis, Muslim, Christian, Buddhist, and Jewish. Even more people stood against the auditorium's walls—a uniquely American kaleidoscope of parents, students, community leaders, scholars, and activists.

I hope these candidates take in how diverse our community really is, I thought. *We are everybody.*

For an hour the candidates— six men and one woman— engaged us in a dialogue.

The time had come for the final question of the night.

Sajida stepped up to the mic, her face bright and her black hair pulled into a ponytail.

I watched the candidates fidget. Facing a child, they knew full well that the pressure was on. How they answered this question would likely make or break their night.

"Hello, my name is Sajida, and I'm in the third grade at PS 169 in Sunset Park, Brooklyn," she began, her voice unwavering and true.

I felt a quiet pride as she confidently launched into her question.

"In June of 2009 the New York City Council passed a

resolution telling the Department of Education to include two major Muslim holidays in the school calendar," she stated. "Even though fifty city council members voted and thought that this was the right thing to do, Mayor Bloomberg said no way. If you are elected mayor, what would you do to make sure that I and the city's other hundred thousand Muslim students don't have to choose between going to school and celebrating our faith?"[16]

All seven candidates broke out in applause.

The leading candidate, Bill de Blasio, declared, "You are a role model to us, young lady."

Christine Quinn, former speaker of the New York City Council, joked, "We are all very glad that you are not running for mayor."[17]

Then one by one every candidate present pledged to formally recognize the two holidays.

YES!

It was a pivotal moment in a campaign that had lasted seven long years—almost as long as my Sajida had been alive. That fall Bill de Blasio was elected mayor of New York City.

A year and a half after that, on March 4, 2015, he held a press conference in Bay Ridge at a school with nearly 50 percent Muslim student enrollment. That's when he announced that both Eid holidays would be incorporated into the New York City public school calendar.

And you'll never guess who was standing right next to him. The now ten-year-old girl who had fearlessly addressed a stage full of politicians and carried us across the finish line!

A few months later Sajida came racing into my bedroom,

whooping and hollering and holding a sheet of paper high in the air.

"Mama," she screamed, "we did it!"

Bouncing from one foot to the other, she handed me the academic calendar for the coming school year, with the dates when public schools would close to celebrate Eid al-Adha and Eid al-Fitr.

Friendship by friendship, conversation by conversation, and collaboration by collaboration, we had amassed a legion of people to stand in solidarity with one another and create change that turned out to be good for everyone.

So I want you to know that no matter your age or how difficult the challenge you face is, ask your friends and family for help when you want to make something important happen. No matter how difficult the battle or how long the fight, when you're standing up for something that's right, by including your allies and refusing to waver, you increase the likelihood that you will prevail. Even if you don't get what you want in that moment, standing up for what you believe in will help you grow stronger and help you prepare for life's next big fight.

CHAPTER 18

Your Fight Is My Fight!

The more I developed relationships with different groups of people, the more I understood how much we have in common. Though on a surface level people may seem to be different, most of us want similar things: to be safe, to be happy, to create a better life. So rather than work on issues only within my own Muslim community, I realized that it made much more sense to fight for everyone's safety and well-being—and ask other people to fight for mine.

So on Father's Day in 2012, I slowly marched up Fifth Avenue with fifty thousand other people participating in the silent march against the New York Police Department's stop-and-frisk policies. We were heading toward Gracie Mansion, the ceremonial home of New York City's mayor, Michael Bloomberg.

Now activists in their own right, my children walked alongside me. Each wore a T-shirt that read:

Walking While Black
Praying While Muslim
ARE NOT CRIMES
#ChangeTheNYPD

"What does it mean?" my daughter Sabreen, then eleven years old, had asked me as she'd pulled her shirt over her head.

"You know how cops are allowed to just stop anyone on the street, and interrogate and search them, even though the people were just walking along minding their own business?" I asked.

"Yes . . . ," she replied.

"Well, that policy is called 'stop-and-frisk,' and it unfairly targets Black people."

"Like the way they detain Muslims for no reason?"

"Exactly," I responded. "And just like they do with Muslims, the police say they only stop and frisk someone when they have a 'reasonable suspicion'"—I made air quotes with my fingers—"that the person might commit a crime."

"How do they know that, though?" Sabreen asked, her eyebrows furrowing.

"Bright girl," I responded, knowing she'd fill in the blanks.

The truth is, many times the police don't know. All too often officers have not received enough training in how to distinguish between people who have committed a crime and people who are innocent. So some police substitute racial profiling or inappropriate stereotypes. Racial profiling involves making a person a suspect or targeting them based on behaviors you assume or imagine exist in their racial or ethnic group.

Racial profiling is sometimes referred to as "ethnic profiling" and can also include profiling people because of their religion or national origin. Such harmful assumptions had caused the occupying forces in Palestine to believe that my uncle Khalo was a threat, caused the New York City police to believe that my schoolmates Ricardo and Mateo were dangerous, and caused the young man in Tamir's classroom to believe that my peace-loving son would ever consider using his math skills to build a bomb.

Most of the time people have no idea that they have absorbed a harmful and inaccurate idea from their family, friends, YouTube, a movie, or society, for example, and are evaluating a group based on a stereotype. That said, there are some people who stereotype intentionally to restrict, offend, or even inflict serious harm upon people whom they interpret as dangerous.

Sadly, some of these stereotypes are taught in police training, which tens of thousands of individual police officers then carry with them, often without knowing it. The officer isn't always the problem; the problem is the training they receive. But either way, these stereotypes make it so innocent and unsuspecting people get harmed, and that isn't right.

In New York City, experts found that even though the police stopped and frisked Black people far more often than white people, Black people were far less likely to be carrying drugs, guns, or other contraband. White people were far more likely to be caught with contraband when police searched them.[18] This practice ruins lives all over the country.

So that's why we decided to participate in the silent march, to make the public more aware of what was happening.

Stopping stop-and-frisk

The march was organized by the time-honored African American civil rights organization the National Association for the Advancement of Colored People—the NAACP—which has been fighting since 1909 for Black people to be safe from racial violence.

As we walked toward Central Park, the starting point, Tamir and Sajida listened intently as other marchers walking with us shared stories about their personal experiences and the shockingly high number of people of color being stopped by the police.

One forty-eight-year-old man who lived in the Bronx described having been stopped ten times. A forty-six-year-old teacher described having been stopped once; his nineteen-year-old son had been stopped three times. The dad feared that the police might escalate the situation.[19]

One victim, David Floyd, was suing the city.

He claimed that in 2008 New York City police officers stopped and searched him and many other Black and Latino men without "reasonable cause." The Fourth Amendment protects people against being searched and having things "seized"—taken—from them unreasonably. And the Fourteenth Amendment guarantees all people equal protection under the law. This stop-and-frisk practice violated both amendments, Mr. Floyd claimed.

"What happened to him?" Sabreen whispered as we walked along Fifty-Ninth Street, the lush greenery of Central Park beside us. We were surrounded by people carrying signs reading END STOP & FRISK and MY SKIN COLOR IS NOT A CRIME, and depicting the name and face of Trayvon Martin, who had been killed in Florida by a neighborhood watch captain earlier in the year.

"Mr. Floyd lived in an apartment building his godmother owned," I told her. "One day a neighbor got locked out, so Mr. Floyd ran upstairs to get the master keys. He wasn't certain which one opened the neighbor's door, so he tried five or six before he found the right one. In the meantime someone had called the cops."

"Why did someone call the police on their neighbor?"

"I don't know, Sabreen," I told her. "But it didn't take long before three police officers showed up demanding to know what was going on. Mr. Floyd told them, but the cops didn't believe him and went ahead and searched them both, assuming wrongly that they had been breaking in. It wasn't until the men showed their IDs that the officers let them go."

During the court case, Mr. Floyd's lawyers presented evidence that the police were stopping far too many Black and Latinx pedestrians. Most police stops took place in Black neighborhoods; in whiter neighborhoods the police only stopped a few people. But the data showed that white people were twice as likely as Black and Latinx people to be carrying illegal items, and more illegal activity had been taking place in whiter neighborhoods than the police had believed.

Earlier, in 2011, the police had detained an African American city council member, Jumaane Williams, and another city official, Kirsten John Foy, as they had attempted to attend a reception at the Brooklyn Museum. The police claimed the men had been walking on a closed sidewalk. Turns out that Mr. Williams had shown the cops his official ID, but officers hadn't believed he was on the city council, because of a stereotype that says Black men on the city council wouldn't wear dreadlocks and that Black men who wore dreadlocks wouldn't be on the city council.

The police threw Williams and Foy to the ground, then manhandled, handcuffed, and detained them.

Clearly the police hadn't realized who they were tangling with. Mr. Foy called his boss, the public advocate Bill de Blasio, who would later become the mayor. Both Williams and Foy were released without being charged.

"If I can't feel safe walking down the street as a New York City Council member," Mr. Williams said, "how is a young Black kid on a street corner in Crown Heights supposed to feel safe?"

Holding police accountable

The similarities between the way the New York Police Department surveilled Muslims and the way it targeted Blacks were clear. The department targeted Black people because of their race; the department targeted Muslims because of their religion. Many Muslims in New York City were also Black. It became clear that by fighting for Black people's civil rights, I was also standing up for the rights of all Muslim people.

But until the AAANY reached out to more than a hundred other groups representing the civil rights of Black, LGBTQ+, Jewish, and Muslim people, as well as educators and labor union members, I didn't know how many other groups had similar concerns.

I learned that as the current laws stood, the police could treat people differently because of their age or gender. Police could stop and question someone simply because they spoke with an accent or wore garments that marked them as being of a particular religion. The police could harass people who were homeless, undocumented, disabled, queer, or transgender. We wanted the police to fight crime, not groups of people, and to stop discriminating against people from all marginalized backgrounds.

Now, just to be clear, I don't think that all police officers misuse their power. However, I do believe that we have a lot of evidence that the policing system in America must be transformed.

As we see on phone-camera videos with shocking frequency, members of law enforcement engage in inappropriate behavior that ranges from being unprofessional, to abusing people, to killing them under questionable circumstances.

But individual police officers are not what I want to fight about. I want to expose, transform, and reimagine what public safety means to us. I want to explore solutions for safety and resilience in our communities that do not require policing. I believe that when our neighborhoods have great schools, ample jobs, access to good healthcare and transportation, and affordable housing and services, this will address crime.

For now the inhumane conduct of police against people results from things like officers having to meet quotas that compel them to make a certain number of arrests each month. If you have to arrest a certain number of people, you are going to be looking for people to arrest. In the process you might be more likely to lean into a stereotype or profile people based upon their race, religion, ethnicity, or national origin. If you fall short of what is required to keep your job, you may be tempted to make up a behavior or situation that results in an arrest.

The way the laws were written in New York, people had no practical remedy when the police violated their rights. We wanted the public to have additional protection.

By standing up for one another, we could solve many problems.

And we did.

After fighting for many months, several of the changes we wanted did become law.

A new police chief changed department policies so that officers targeted Black and Brown communities less. And contrary to what the naysayers warned, the city's crime rate didn't go up.[20]

Within months the police shut down a unit of the NYPD that had been tasked with spying on Muslim communities.

CHAPTER 19

Social Justice Voltron Unite!

We can't—and we shouldn't expect to—do everything by ourselves. Our friends are our greatest allies.

The more I saw all the things that various communities had in common, the stronger my relationships with those allies grew. So did my friendships with some of their leaders.

Enter Carmen and Tamika.

For all my life as an activist, they had always been there—Carmen, a small-framed Chicana with gentle eyes, and Tamika, a petite, fiery African American woman. We occupied the same rooms, marched in the same protests, and raised our voices for the same causes.

Funny that no one had ever thought to introduce us. Everyone had probably assumed we already knew one another. And in a way they were right. As we stood up for equality and fairness in different ways, we ended up in the same spaces and got to know each other's work. I would see their passion and humanity; I would admire how deeply they cared about the people they fought for.

But I had no idea that one day the three of us would develop an unbreakable friendship—a "social justice Voltron," as Carmen calls us. By loving and supporting one another and working jointly, we accomplish a tremendous amount together and never feel alone.

Three is company

Carmen grew up in Oxnard, California, in a largely Latinx farm town located outside Los Angeles. When she was seventeen, her sister Patricia was killed in a car accident. Though the family suspected that gangs might have been involved, when the police asked her father if he wanted to press charges against the driver, he declined.

"My grief is hard enough," he said. "I would never take another mother's child away."

Carmen was passionate about improving opportunities for young, low-income Chicanos. When you grow up poor, experience hunger, go to substandard schools, have a hard time finding a job, and struggle to participate in mainstream society, you're more likely to become involved in a gang. Gangs, in turn, increase your odds of tangling with police, getting arrested, and possibly being jailed.

She also had beliefs about police reform that were similar to mine. Carmen's brother was "a good guy" who tried to do the right things. Yet the police would stop and frisk him week after week. After college she became a youth probation officer, working with youth who'd gotten into trouble, to help them stay out of jail.

Back in my neck of the woods, Tamika grew up in Harlem, New York, where her parents helped the Reverend Al Sharpton found the National Action Network (NAN), a civil rights organization that helps ensure that all Americans have an equal opportunity in our society. She marched in protests since she was an eleven-year-old student in Catholic school.

When Tamika was nineteen, the police gunned down an African Muslim immigrant named Amadou Diallo as he was returning to his home in the Bronx. The officers claimed they mistook Mr. Diallo for a suspect in a year-old crime. All the cops were wearing street clothes, not uniforms, and a witness testified that they didn't identify themselves. Then for some inexplicable reason, they shot forty-one bullets at Mr. Diallo; nineteen hit him. The investigation found that Diallo was reaching for his wallet when the police shot him. He was unarmed.

At that point Tamika began pushing for police reform. But you don't get involved in a cause like this thinking that you'll experience gun violence yourself. Then her son's father was shot and killed. At that point Tamika joined in the fight against gun violence and the fight for gun safety and for ending overly aggressive policing of communities of color. In 2011 she became the youngest ever executive director of NAN.

The intense tragedies that Carmen, Tamika, and I experienced at a young age changed us. Our losses made us hyperaware of our responsibility to care for and protect people in our communities. But little did we know that God would bring us together.

In 2008, Carmen moved to New York to become a national organizer for the racial and social justice organization the Gathering for Justice, founded by the legendary singer, actor, and activist Harry Belafonte. Back when he was growing up in the Caribbean, when some of the island nations had still been British colonies, Mr. Belafonte had witnessed the British authorities there oppressing the Black residents. And though he went on to become a famous actor and music sensation, he never forgot what he'd seen. During the 1950s he became a close friend of Dr. Martin Luther King. He also became a strong voice for and financial backer of the civil rights movement, and an international humanitarian and fierce advocate all over the world.

By 2010 he'd become revered as a community elder, mentoring, guiding, and developing young leaders. His organization the Gathering for Justice creates change by using the nonviolent tactics Dr. King made popular. It teaches that we can resist evil and combat hate and even violence by activating the power of love.

"Defeat is never an option," he told about twenty community activists one evening when he'd invited us to gather in the organization's offices. Even though he was well into his eighties, Mr. Belafonte remained energetic and lively. His voice was raspy and bore the slightest waver, but his eyes danced with fire!

That night his grace, authority, and humanity felt like an infinite fountain of love, pouring life into us all.

During the civil rights movement, people repeatedly marched for freedom and equality so that we would have the right to vote and raise our voices, he told us in his whispery voice.

I believed Mr. Belafonte with all my heart. I hung on to each one of his words, feeling privileged that he believed in us to carry on that struggle. I was in awe of his commitment— fifty years later it still had not dimmed. He then poured that passion into Carmen.

"Always meet hate with love," she would remind us in her nonviolence trainings. "Never allow other people's poison to find its way inside you. Instead be a serene mirror for the world, trusting that actions undertaken in good faith will have good outcomes."

Over the years, Carmen collaborated with NAN, AAANY, and various other civil rights groups as we partnered to reform our criminal justice system.

But Carmen, Tamika, and I wouldn't truly see the connections between each of our efforts until two additional tragedies took place.

When a video goes viral

On July 17, 2014, police stopped a man named Eric Garner, a husband, father of six, and grandfather in Staten Island, New York. They suspected he'd been selling "loosies"—single cigarettes. In some lower-income neighborhoods people can't afford to pay thirteen dollars for a pack of cigarettes, so some people sell loosies for fifty cents. It's against the law because the sellers don't pay cigarette taxes, but it's a way to make a little money. Getting caught is a low-level offense called a misdemeanor, and the punishment is a few hundred dollars.

When police approached Mr. Garner, he was chatting with a twenty-two-year-old man, Ramsey Orta. Knowing how some police harass Black people, Mr. Orta quietly started filming. In the video you see Mr. Garner tell the cops, who are white, that he isn't feeling well and is sick and tired of them always hassling him. (Later we would learn that the police had arrested Mr. Garner several times for minor infractions, such as selling loosies and driving without his license.)

Officer Daniel Pantaleo tried to handcuff Mr. Garner.

"Don't touch me, man," Mr. Garner said, and walked away.

Then Officer Pantaleo and his partner, Officer Justin D'Amico, tackled Mr. Garner. Officer Pantaleo wrapped his arm around Garner's neck and put him in a dangerous choke hold position that the NYPD had banned, while pressing Mr. Garner's face into the ground.

"I can't breathe. I can't breathe," Mr. Garner gasped, not once, not twice, but *eleven* times. Still Officer Pantaleo did not release his hold until Garner's body slumped and went still.

At that point the cops began chasing away the crowd of witnesses who had gathered around.

By then Mr. Garner had lost consciousness. He died an hour later at the hospital.

Mr. Orta posted his video on the internet. You know what

happened next, right? It went viral. That's when the entire world could witness this police killing, hearing Mr. Garner moan, "I can't breathe. I can't breathe."

Later the city medical examiner would call Mr. Garner's death a homicide, which means that someone's intentional actions are what caused his death.

Standing in solidarity

I can't breathe.

I felt Eric Garner's final three words in the pit of my stomach as I watched the video again and again, remembering how Basemah had used them as she'd lain dying.

Why didn't Officer Pantaleo immediately let go of Garner's throat? The proof that three officers sworn to protect and serve the public had suffocated Garner was agonizing to witness.

I.

Can't.

Breathe.

Basemah's voice intermingled with Mr. Garner's. I felt like she was urging me to think bigger. To expand my mission and activism. To encourage Muslims to connect with our allies and turn out for the protests throughout the city to speak out against Mr. Garner's death.

But even as I lent my voice to these calls for justice, a second senseless execution of a Black man by a white police officer sparked further sorrow and outrage.

On August 9, 2014, Michael Brown, an eighteen-year-old

about to begin his first semester in college, was walking to his grandmother's house with a friend in Ferguson, Missouri. As these young men ambled down Canfield Drive, Officer Darren Wilson pulled up in his police cruiser and told them to walk on the sidewalk.

Witnesses don't completely agree about what happened next.

Officer Wilson says Brown punched him and then ran, once Wilson pulled his gun out and started shooting. Some witnesses say Brown did not assault the officer. They say he ran from the cruiser after the cop started firing, then turned around and put his hands in the air and yelled, "Don't shoot!" These witnesses claim that Officer Wilson kept on squeezing the trigger, firing twelve shots in all. Six entered Brown's body.

Michael Brown didn't have a gun, yet this unarmed young Black man was executed in the middle of the street in the full light of day. To add insult to injury, as crowds gathered, the police let his body lie in the street for four hours as the August sun blazed down on him.

Okay, I knew this kind of incident happened a lot in Palestine. How was it also happening in America?

My Tamir was about the same age as Michael Brown. My heart clenched when I imagined how I might feel if this had happened to him. That's when I began to understand that these same types of issues were happening all around the country—from Staten Island, New York; to Ferguson, Missouri; to Oxnard, California. We needed to mobilize on a national level, from sea to shining sea.

The next week I flew to Ferguson. It felt right for me,

an American Muslim woman who wears a hijab, to stand in solidarity with protesters marching for Black lives.

But I have to admit that I was shocked by what I saw in Ferguson.

As people protested peacefully, the government showed up with SWAT teams, military weapons, armored tanks, and tear gas. I'd seen scenes like this when our military had deployed to places like Iraq and Afghanistan. But this was a suburb in America's heartland.

We're deploying the military against our own citizens? I thought.

America is the land of the free, the home of the brave A government of the people, by the people, for the people. Or is it?

"No justice, no peace," we chanted, exercising our First Amendment right to free speech as our eyes burned and we choked on the tear gas that law enforcement officers had fired into the crowd. I was stunned to experience how much Ferguson looked like Palestine. (Today I'm a bit embarrassed to admit just how incredulous I was. The Black activists seemed not to be surprised.)

After this experience I partnered with another Muslim leader to unite the many groups of Muslims around the United States. Together we founded the group Muslims for Ferguson. Our goal was to encourage Muslim Americans to embrace the fight against police brutality as a top priority.

Using hashtags like #MuslimsForFerguson, Muslim people from Palestine and all over the world began tweeting their support for the Ferguson activists.

"Hamde Abu tells #Ferguson that #Palestine knows what it means to be shot for your ethnicity," Rana Nazzal wrote of the Palestinian activist holding up a sign expressing thoughts similar to those she'd tweeted.[21]

Some shared directly from their own experiences as Israeli forces attacked the residents of Palestine that summer.

"Always make sure to run against the wind / to keep calm when you're teargassed, the pain will pass, don't rub your eyes! #Ferguson Solidarity," Palestinian journalist and activist Mariam Barghouti tweeted from the West Bank, also advising protesters to rinse their eyes with milk.

"And of course DON'T wash your eyes with water," replied Rajai Abukhalil. He also tweeted: "Don't Keep much distance from the Police, if you're close to them they can't tear Gas. To #Ferguson from #Palestine."[22]

Even journalists used social media to share pictures showing the similarities between the uprising in Ferguson and Arab protests against oppression.[23] Barghouti also posted photos pointing out that the same Pennsylvania-based company had provided the tear gas that was being used in both Ferguson and Palestine.[24]

Palestinian Americans joined in as well. The US branch of the Palestinian Youth Movement published a statement that included these words:

> Like Black and Brown communities righteously struggling against incarceration and subjugation, Palestinians righteously resist their annihilation and are systematically and illegally held captive

in Israeli prisons. Like Black and Brown communities displaced by gentrification and discriminatory laws and lending, Palestinian homes are confiscated and our lands annexed daily to build illegal and exclusive Jewish-only settlements. Like Black and Brown communities, Palestinians, African and Asian migrants living and working in the State of Israel suffer as second and third class citizens under an apartheid legal system.

Activist Bassem Masri livestreamed from Ferguson and was even arrested. Later he wrote,

As the son of immigrant small business owners from Palestine, I was taught to believe in the American dream of freedom, liberty and the white picket fence. This past summer has shattered this belief. The dream doesn't apply to certain people in our society.

When Mike Brown was murdered in Ferguson my people in Gaza were being slaughtered by Israel in Operation Protective Edge. The timing of the two events woke up a lot of people. When Mike was killed, much of the media started demonizing him and the protestors, often the same sources that blamed Palestinians for their own deaths in Gaza. People naturally saw the connections.[25]

This type of sharing made clear the similarities in our oppression.

I remember one photo of a Palestinian graffiti artist spray-painting FROM FERGUSON TO PALESTINE—RESISTANCE IS NOT A CRIME. END RACISM NOW! ♥ STL–PSC.[26]

Before long, anti-oppression organizers the Dream Defenders and BLM members traveled to Palestine to meet with grassroots leaders and discuss how the two struggles against violence and oppression were closely related to each other.

Waking up

People marched arm in arm though the streets of Ferguson, shouting together, crying together, supporting one another, rinsing out each other's eyes and choking on the same tear gas, feeling afraid but also powerful. Together. My feet ached for sure, but with each story I heard and every step forward I trudged, I understood more deeply how a change for one brings change for all. My heart began to swell with the feeling of power we have when people unite to fight injustice.

I was growing into someone who doesn't let fear stop her, but I'm not gonna lie—staring down military tanks and officers wearing helmets and carrying shields is no joke. There were times when my heart was racing and my knees were knocking.

In those moments of great anxiety, it became clear that not all Americans grieve for people we see as "other." My eyes were opened wide to the reality that we tend to identify more with people we see as similar to us. But interacting with so many diverse people had taught me that human beings want very similar things for our lives, families, and children. When we "other," we become ignorant to the reality that when one person experiences injustice, everyone gets harmed. When we see some people as less deserving than we are, we don't feel one another's pain equally—which makes it seem like that other person's suffering okay.

That November, a Missouri grand jury determined that Michael Brown's killer, Officer Darren Wilson, hadn't broken a law.

Just one week later in New York, the courts decided not to charge Officer Pantaleo for Eric Garner's death.

All across the nation people of conscience were heart-broken and angry. On college campuses students staged "die-ins," where they lay on the ground reenacting that part of the men's deaths.

This brings me to Tamika and Carmen.

Back in New York the three of us came together to help organize rallies to protest injustice, to get people's attention and serve notice to the powerful that many Americans are fed up and refuse to accept police violence anymore. We helped organize demonstrations that blocked highways around New York City, as other protesters poured into Macy's department store and lay themselves down in the aisles. A few blocks away in Bryant Park, people lay shoulder to shoulder on the ground on a rainy night, holding signs that echoed Garner's last words: "I can't breathe."

Everyday people transformed themselves into citizen

journalists, using their cell phones to record and upload events to platforms such as Twitter, Facebook, and YouTube. Actions unfolded so quickly and so universally that the mainstream media couldn't keep up.

An alliance of friends

During this time new groups of activists began to collaborate. I was invited to join the Justice League NYC, an alliance of individuals coming together to spark an intergenerational movement for nonviolent social change.

Many deep problems take decades to solve, and injustice in the United States is definitely one of them. Police violence toward innocent people has been happening for generations, so it helps to have mentors, and people older, wiser, and more experienced than you who have been fighting the battle longer, to have your back, and who will support your vision and provide guidance.

Our first action would take place in early December. We would stage a mass protest called the Royal Shutdown outside Brooklyn's Barclays Center arena, where Prince William and Kate Middleton would be sitting courtside at a Cleveland Cavaliers–Brooklyn Nets game.

On that cold night in December 2014, hundreds of us stood outside the arena chanting, "I can't breathe" and "All I want for Christmas is to live" and "How do you spell 'racist'? N-Y-P-D!" Some of us even wore plastic crowns to make a visual statement of how absurd it was for the press to preoccupy itself with a royal visit when police were killing people in the streets. We also staged a die-in, where protesters lay down on the pavement, a sea of bodies side by side in the night, in complete silence for half an hour. Police scanners crackled, the street traffic hummed, press photographers' camera shutters click-click-clicked, as citizens buzzed about recording our protest. Inside the arena, Jay-Z had signed on as one of our allies. He delivered black T-shirts with the words *I CAN'T BREATHE* to the players. The Cavs' star player, LeBron James, and several others pulled them on at halftime.

By coming together as an alliance of friends—and by mixing our political messages with entertainment and culture—we expanded our impact by attracting young people of color who understood us and trusted us. But to tell you the truth: staying positive was a struggle. We needed Mr. Belafonte's support so that we didn't lose hope.

One day Mr. B. told twenty Justice League members several stories from his youth.

"Defeat is not an option," he had said, and I believed him with all my heart.

Among the powerful stories he told us that day, we learned about the march from Selma to Montgomery, Alabama. In March 1965 a march was supposed to go from Selma to the state capital, Montgomery, to protest laws, regulations, literacy tests, and other forms of racial intimidation intended to keep Black Americans from voting. At that time in Selma there was both an active voting rights movement and a protest against the police murder of an unarmed Black activist and church deacon, Jimmie Lee Jackson.

The first time they tried to march, the mostly Black contingent of protesters—led by a minister, Hosea Williams, and twenty-five-year-old John Lewis, who would later become an influential congressman—crossed the Edmund Pettus Bridge leaving Selma. But they were met by Alabama state troopers, other representatives of law enforcement, and citizens—all of whom were white and some of whom were on horseback—who tear-gassed the marchers, beat them with billy clubs and whips, and threatened them with snarling dogs. In fact, the cops beat John Lewis so badly that they fractured his skull.[27] They clubbed another marcher, Amelia Boynton, unconscious.[28]

Television cameras broadcasted the violence all around the world—shaming Alabama and the nation. The day went down in infamy as "Bloody Sunday." Afterward, all around the nation people held sit-ins, blocked traffic, and engaged in other forms of peaceful protest to show their solidarity.

No matter what law enforcement did, the Selma protesters practiced nonviolence. Nonviolence doesn't just mean that you don't hit people back; it involves actively resisting evil and courageously combatting hate and violence with the power of love, by looking people in their eyes lovingly as they hurl slurs, attempt to hurt you, or even as they physically attack you.

Two days later the Selma protesters began the march a second time. This time they walked across the bridge to the site of the attack, prayed, and then turned back to Selma. Behind the scenes a federal court judge was planning on issuing a restraining order to prevent the march. Though Dr. King wanted to march without protection, it was necessary if the protestors were to continue their cause. Nevertheless, that night in Selma a white mob beat to death a white minister, Rev. James Reeb, who had traveled from Boston to participate in the march.

Almost two weeks later the federal government sent in the National Guard, FBI, and federal marshals to protect the marchers, and more than two thousand people set out to walk the fifty-four-mile journey along Highway 80 to Montgomery to challenge the laws and customs of racial segregation so that African Americans could freely vote—a crowd that eventually swelled to twenty-five thousand.[29] Mr. Belafonte used his star power to bring some of the nation's most celebrated artists—from gospel singer Mahalia Jackson to conductor Leonard Bernstein; from jazz great Nina Simone to folk singer Joan Baez; to folk singer Pete Seeger—to support the cause of racial justice.

The marchers were exhausted, Mr. Belafonte told us, but the music restored their souls.

"There was no other choice but to keep going," he said. "Defeat is never an option."

He then looked around the room, seeming to hold each of us in his gaze. "All of you here have inherited the mantle from the ones who marched then, and we are all counting on you."

In This Together: How to Be a Great Activist and Ally

You don't have to be the next Dr. Martin Luther King Jr., Congressman John Lewis, Tamika Mallory, or former football great Colin Kaepernick to be a great activist.

You are an activist when you positively impact the life of just one person. Here are some tips to remind you of how you can be an activist and ally in your everyday life:

• Be kind and respectful to everyone, no matter who they are, what they look like, or what they believe in. Treat others how you want to be treated.

• Stand up when you see that someone else is being mistreated. Speak up when you see something wrong in your school or community.

• Read books and watch documentaries to help you better understand people and their different experiences.

• Learn American history from a multicultural perspective so that humanity can go forward, not backward. Knowledge is power.

• Remind yourself that we're all in this together. If one of us is hurting, all of us are hurting.

• You belong to the generation that will change the world. That change starts with you. You are an activist— we are not here to be bystanders.

CHAPTER 20

#March2Justice

A month later the same Justice League group gathered in Mr. B.'s office again. He wasn't present and we were feeling glum.

"The police are just killing us and getting away with it," Tamika exclaimed, throwing out her hands in frustration. "This is not justice. We have to make people pay attention."

That afternoon we decided to hold our own march—this time from New York City to Washington, DC. We would call it the #March2Justice.

We set our step-off date for April 13, 2015. That year marked the fiftieth anniversary of Bloody Sunday and forty-seven years since the assassination of Dr. King. (It is hard to believe that all these years later we are still marching for Black lives to be safe from police violence and for Black people to feel valued.) We decided that along the way we would register voters, since the 2016 presidential race was heating up. We planned daily morning and evening rallies to raise awareness of police violence upon communities of color. Each evening, we would take buses from the stopping point of that day's leg of the journey to wherever we would sleep that night. And we would spend the night in churches, mosques, temples, schools, and community centers along the way.

When we arrived in Washington, we would deliver to members of Congress the three-point justice package we'd developed. The package consisted of the End Racial Profiling Act, a Stop Militarizating Law Enforcement Act, and a Juvenile Justice and Delinquency Prevention Act. Several congressional representatives even committed to bringing our proposals to the floor so they could be debated and voted on.

Finally, in the spirit that Mr. Belafonte had described, we planned to gather on the lawn of the United States Capitol, where like-minded artists could perform and we leaders fighting for justice would speak.

Foot soldiers for justice

At nine a.m. on April 13, one hundred people set off from Staten Island. They were Christian, Muslim, Jewish, agnostic, and atheist; college students, artists, and musicians; PTA moms and soccer dads, ministers, city council members, attorneys, and labor unionists; people who had formerly been incarcerated; community organizers; and even a few long-time foot soldiers from the civil rights movement. Most were young college students. Three quarters of our group were African American.

Our youngest marcher, Skylar Shafer, was a white sixteen-year-old from Litchfield, Connecticut. She had signed up for the march as an advocate for children who had grown up during a war.

Our oldest, sixty-four-year-old Bruce Richard, had been an activist since a police officer had lifted him overhead and slammed him to the ground back when Mr. Bruce was only twelve.

The crime?

He and his cousins had kept singing doo-wop songs after the officer had told them to stop.

Another marcher, twenty-two-year-old Shana Salzberg, carried a picture of her grandfather, who had survived the Holocaust, as her inspiration. Though there were hundreds of stories and reasons for joining, every one of us who pulled on our walking shoes and thick black Justice League NYC sweatshirts that chilly morning understood that we were marching to save lives.

At the end of day three, we arrived in Philadelphia, where we stayed at the Al-Hidaya mosque. "Hidaya" means "guidance" or "showing the way." In Islam, guidance is a gift from God.[30]

"We are so honored you are here," the imam said in welcome. "I want you to remember that this house belongs to God, and you are all God's creations, so this is your house tonight. I ask you to treat this house like it is your home."

With its crystal chandeliers, expansive rooms, colorful mosaics, kitchen, and hot showers, Al-Hidaya was a beautiful home where we could rest our heads. Almost none of the marchers had been in a mosque before, but after they had eaten their fill of the steak, chicken, rice, vegetables, and dessert that the mosque had provided, they began sweeping and cleaning up inside and out.

As they swept outside, one of the Justice League members, an Iranian filmmaker named Rameen, noticed a black car with tinted windows parked across the street with two men sitting inside. He also noticed a drone flying back and forth over the mosque's gold dome.

Law enforcement officers were surveilling the mosque and our little band of marchers! A lot of the kids were shocked, but sadly this is the reality that many Muslims endure—and especially those who are Black or Brown.

The college kids stayed up late that night, talking with the Muslims in our group and members of the mosque about their experiences in America after 9/11. This was their first experience understanding how vulnerable you feel when you know that government agents are watching you—and not for your protection but because they see you as a potential enemy.

Though we were marching to protest the ways law enforcement criminalized communities of color, it was also becoming increasingly clear how closely woven the movement for Black lives was with Muslims' struggle. It was beautiful to watch people make those connections. Everyone could see that we're all in this together.

I woke up the next morning at five fifteen, to the melodic voice of the imam reciting the adhan, the call to prayer, over the loudspeakers. I sat on my air mattress with my eyes closed, listening to the call—the sound soft and lyrical, the song of a nightingale, a wailing. The haunting refrain almost brought me to tears. Around me people started stirring, sitting up, rubbing their eyes.

"What's that?" they asked. "What's going on?"

I shared with them what the imam was doing and translated from Arabic to English:

> God is the greatest.
> I testify that there is no God but Allah.
> Muhammad is the messenger of God.
> Come to prayer. . . .

Now everyone listened, entranced by the sheer beauty of the imam's voice and the way the sounds reverberated in their heart. Some bowed their heads and said their own prayers, while others stared up at the ceiling or down at their hands, respectful and silent.

A few hours later, as we loaded back into our bus to continue our travels, the imam gave us crates of bananas, oranges, and bottled water.

"We are so grateful for the work you are doing on behalf of all of us," he said. Then we pulled out of the parking lot past the unidentified black car still sitting there.

I can't tell you how grateful I felt for our experience at Al-Hidaya. I was thankful that the first experience the students and other non-Muslims in our group had had inside a mosque had been warm. I felt a secret pride too because the people at Al-Hidaya had been Palestinian immigrants. Many people in our society don't trust them to carry a book bag without worrying that they might be a terrorist. In spite of that, they had generously invited busloads of Black and Brown people of different faiths to come inside their holy space. Then they had trusted the visitors to treat the space like their home.

These kinds of cross-cultural experiences reduce the odds that people will hate one another. I have no doubt that if any students who visited Al-Hidaya ever faced Islamophobia, they would speak up.

"Oh no!" they would say. "I *know* Muslims. They welcomed us into their mosque. They fed and cared for us. You are so wrong about them."

Knowing this gave me tremendous peace as we set off on the next leg of our march.

Hate meets love

"White power. Get off my street!" one man hollered as he roared by in his pickup truck.

"Go get a job," yelled another.

"Whoa, the racists are out," one of the marchers exclaimed, sounding more than a little worried. I'm not gonna lie, we were vulnerable out there on the road. It was nerve-wracking.

"Don't pay them any attention," I instructed, channeling Carmen's words and the strength of all of our elders. "Just keep walking and keep your eyes facing forward and toward each other. Engaging with them makes them feel more powerful. Keep talking to each other normally and emanate the energy of love."

I don't know what to tell you—racist people still exist.

We were walking Route 1 in rural Pennsylvania just north of the Maryland border. On this part of our trip, we trudged through towns where every house had a Confederate flag fluttering on a flagpole or hanging in a window. Even though we were still north of the Mason-Dixon Line, there were Confederate flags on every car and pickup truck, every strip mall and billboard, and even every church sign. To some white people, the Confederate flag represents their Southern heritage.[31] But it also symbolizes white Southerners' attempts to maintain slavery, Jim Crow racial segregation, white supremacy, and racial violence. So lots of other people—and particularly African Americans—find the flag offensive and threatening.

"Our ancestors were strong and powerful," Carmen reminded the marchers. "They are all around us. Everything's going to be all right."

A purple car with a painted sign that read KUPKAKEKART drove by.

"Whoa, did you see that?" one of the Black marchers asked. "I wonder if that person is in the Ku Klux Klan." The Klan is an all-white terrorist organization with a long history of violence toward Black people in particular.[32]

"For God's sake!" I exclaimed. "No doubt."

The meaning of the three capitalized Ks came through loud and clear. Clearly the Klan was alive and well in this community. Just beyond the border lay the town of Rising Sun, the Klan's regional headquarters. We found ourselves with no police protection of any kind, and with many very hostile townspeople.

Countless drivers leaned out of their cars and yelled the N-word at us, their faces contorted into masks of hate. Some others pulled over close enough to blow exhaust smoke at us while flipping us the bird and screaming profanity. Obviously I'm not Black, but I wear a hijab. So I knew darn well that many of those people didn't like me, either. Some drivers would form their hands into the shape of a gun, take aim, and pretend to shoot us.

It was a good thing that Carmen had trained us in the principles of nonviolence and civil disobedience.

Mercifully, even though we felt exposed as we marched through that part of Pennsylvania, no one perpetrated physical violence against us that day. But you feel it when people yell ugly racist comments and other vulgarities at you for several hours. Even with our training and Carmen's loving reminders, psychologically it wore us down. I'm not gonna lie. Klan country was tense.

A torrent of sorrow

That evening we boarded buses to Lincoln University, a historically Black college near Oxford, Pennsylvania. Lincoln was founded in 1854 to educate young Black men during a time when many white people in the North would not admit Black people to schools, and in the South it was illegal to educate Black people. Lincoln was also the first historically Black institution to offer its graduates a college degree. Today people of all races and genders get educated there.

That night at Lincoln was our lowest moment. The day

had been hardest on the young Black marchers. Now safe, they released some of the tears they'd been forced to suppress in order to live in a hateful world each day. They held one another and wiped one another's tears. Shattered, some of the young people fell to their knees bawling, unable to bear the great weight any longer.

Always a healer, Carmen became our empathetic big sister and earth mother. She gathered everyone into a huddle and had us hold one another. We laced our arms across each other's backs, bowed our heads in a tight circle, and touched our foreheads together.

"God loves you all," she kept saying in her soft, soothing, musical voice. "You are so worthy, every single one of you, and you are so loved."

She just kept affirming us in that way, especially the students, whose heartache was greatest.

"We are all here for you. We are all here together," she told them. "You are wholeheartedly loved. God is right here among us, holding you up. Remember who you are, and why you are here. You are a warrior for justice, and everyone is so grateful for your courage, your spirit, your leadership, your love."

Tamika and I call this "Carmen talk," because Carmen has this way of taking your broken pieces and making you feel whole again. That night as the tears flowed, she hugged every single person individually. Then she lit some sage to cleanse the air and to promote healing and wisdom.

"May our angels manifest our highest good, watch over and protect us," she prayed. "God, I ask that you bring us through the journey with our hearts filled to overflowing with nothing but peace and love."

Cracked open

When you try to make change, you will face opposition. But it is important not to let those who oppose you stop you.

So we cried our tears, dried them, and the next day continued our journey down Route 1, this day breathing in the fresh country air and enjoying the grassy green hills and farmhouses, some of which dated back to the colonial era.

Walking for hours alongside so many people who had been directly affected by encounters with police gave me a new understanding of what life is like for many African Americans. In the cities and towns that we passed through, we stopped to listen to residents' stories. Back in Philadelphia, Tanya Brown-Dickerson recalled the night police shot her twenty-six-year-old son, Brandon Tate-Brown, in the back of the head during a traffic stop. Along the way I heard many other accounts of brothers, uncles, fathers, sons, mothers, daughters who had been brutalized by police; terrible stories about stop-and-frisks; and the horror the Black community faces each time they watch young Black people such as Akai Gurley, Rekia Boyd, Ramarley Graham, Renisha McBride, Jordan Davis, and Tamir Rice being cut down in their prime.

Before I'd set off on the march, I'd thought I understood the need for the Black Lives Matter movement. But I was really getting an education I'd never received before. It wasn't until that pilgrimage with Black people that I began to grasp BLM's importance in a much deeper way. The animosity we encountered helped me understand more deeply how many Black people experience hatred every day, just as their parents and grandparents had. And though it's bad enough that Muslims are surveilled and harassed, not many non-Black Muslims die in police custody.

Hearing the firsthand experiences of my fellow justice warriors in the African American community really transformed me.

"Our demand is simple," many Black Lives Matter activists explained. "Stop killing us."

I felt like all the notions I'd been socialized to believe about freedom and justice in America were being cracked open so that the truth could be exposed. With each passing day I became clearer and clearer about the struggles that all oppressed people experience—whether they live in El Bireh or in Brooklyn or in Harlem, Staten Island, Ferguson, Oxnard, or beyond. With each mile we walked I became more determined that we all work together. For me there was no turning back.

On day six, a Saturday, we started getting close to Baltimore. By then everyone on the march felt bonded. We slept that night at the Empowerment Temple church, home to one of the largest African Methodist Episcopal congregations in the country. The following morning we attended Sunday services led by Pastor Jamal Bryant. Toward the end of his sermon our cell phones began vibrating. With so many notifications going off at once, we started peeking at our screens— and that's how we learned that Freddie Gray had just died, in west Baltimore, just a few miles away.

Changing directions

Twenty-five-year-old Freddie Carlos Gray Jr. had lived with his twin sister in a really big housing project in one of Baltimore's poorest neighborhoods. On April 12, 2015, the day before we'd set off on our march, six Baltimore police officers had arrested him for possession of a pocket-knife that turned out to not even be illegal. Community members who witnessed the arrest claimed that the cops handcuffed Freddie, roughed him up pretty badly, and then shoved him into a police van. By the time the van got to the police station, he had spinal cord injuries and was barely alive.

Freddie died that morning while we were worshipping at church.

Now, as services ended and the church emptied, our group huddled in the parking lot to discuss how to respond.

"I think we should head to Baltimore," Tamika decided. "Let's support this community during this moment of tremendous pain."

We stood with the community as they protested in the street outside the police precinct.

"Justice for Freddie Gray!" some cried.

"Freddie was my brother! You murdered him!" a man shouted, his arms around a woman who was crumpled against him, her face pressed into his shoulder.

Amid the cries, the chants, the sobbing, and the yelling, we mixed with the crowd, introducing ourselves, explaining that we had been marching against police brutality when we'd heard about Freddie. "We're here to stand with you," we said. "We want justice for Freddie too."

After a little while one of the police officers involved with Freddie's arrest sprinted from the station to his car. The crowd surged around his vehicle, banging on his windows, rocking the car, howling at him with rage and pain. I looked around wildly, trying to figure out what to do, but before anyone realized what was happening, Tamika squeezed her little body through the crowd of mostly men, all of them bigger than she was. The next thing I knew, she was standing with her back against the policeman's car. I'm not gonna lie. I was frightened. But I trusted that Tamika knew what she was doing.

"I need you all to back up off this car right now!" she yelled over the shouts and cries, raising her hands over her head to command more space. "If you love Freddie Gray, and I know you do, then you want justice for Freddie Gray, but this is not the way! If you love Freddie Gray, and I know you do, you do not want to be behind bars today! You are worth more than that. Freddie would not be proud of you if something happens to this police officer. But let me be very clear, I'm not here trying to protect people who don't care about us, who don't protect us. I'm trying to protect you! You are the ones who matter to me! And I'm standing here right now trying to make sure what happened to Freddie Gray won't happen to you!"

My God, I was in awe of her—all 120 pounds of ferocious courage. I could hardly believe what she was doing, with absolutely no thought for her own safety. As far as Tamika was concerned, these men were her brothers; these were her people. She'd grown up with them, organized rallies with them, and knew that their rage in this moment was sorrow. So she talked to them as if she were talking to her own family, with fierce empathy and sisterly love.

"I am not protecting this police officer!" she repeated, shouting to be heard above the crowd. "I am here to protect you! I know you're angry and I want you to be angry, but right now we need to let this police officer go. We don't need more dead Black men out here in these streets, because we've got work to do!"

It was extraordinary to see the men's faces soften as they recognized how much Tamika cared about them, how much she understood them, to behold her instinctive leadership. Her body was so small, yet she commanded that crowd with such power and eloquence. She made them feel her love. "You matter to me," she kept saying. "I'm standing here for you."

That afternoon in the western district of Baltimore was yet another pivotal moment on our march. I had witnessed Carmen's motherly leadership in the chapel at Lincoln University, and now I was seeing Tamika's fiery integrity and bedrock commitment to the people she fought for every single day. These two women put everything on the line in the fight for justice, and I felt privileged to stand with them.

In the weeks that followed we would learn that the police officers who'd arrested Freddie hadn't put a seat belt on him. As the driver had veered and swerved and turned corners on the city's streets, Freddie had gotten thrown around in the back—some say on purpose. Because he'd been handcuffed, he'd been unable to use his arms and hands to protect his head. His death was ruled a homicide, caused because officers hadn't followed department policy of putting a seat belt on the person they'd arrested.

Even worse, we learned that Freddie Gray shouldn't have been in police custody at all. He hadn't pulled out his knife or brandished it in any way. Later all six police officers would be charged with crimes, but eventually all would be either declared innocent or set free.

How can the police kill so many Black people and get away with it in so many parts of the country? I wondered. Perhaps these police officers hadn't broken the law, but their behavior had been immoral and unjust. The laws were unjust. Something about policing was unjust, particularly when Black and Brown people were involved.

Clearly we would need to change a lot of laws to reform the culture of policing—and to help keep honest and honorable police officers from being trained inadequately and thrust into situations that they haven't been properly prepared to handle.

Redeeming the soul of America

Later that day we reached Washington, DC, where we slept inside the historic Masjid Muhammad, also known as "the Nation's Mosque," where Malcolm X, whose life had inspired me when I was a high school student, had once prayed and preached.[33]

On Tuesday, April 20, we strode toward the expansive, green West Lawn of the United States Capitol. Our feet ached and our backs hurt, and many of us were hoarse. But our chants of "I can't breathe" and "Hands up, don't shoot" echoed powerfully in the streets.

"Thank you for joining us. It's great to have you with us," we exclaimed as other groups joined the last leg of our journey— gun-violence survivors; immigrant-rights advocates; women's groups; Black Lives Matter activists; LGBTQ+, Latinx, and Asian American organizations; and other everyday Americans. Our #March2Justice swelled from a hundred hardy souls who had walked 250 miles to some two thousand strong.

"We're happy to be here," they responded. "Thank you for organizing the march and inviting us to participate."

Once we reached the Capitol stage, Congressman John Lewis and other leaders, actors, and musicians joined us. A diverse community of people spoke, artists performed, and we presented our three-point justice package to members of the congressional Black, Hispanic, and Asian caucuses.

A twelve-year-old girl named Heaven brought us to tears as she told us about her father, Bobby Gross, who had been gunned down by the DC Metro Transit Police just weeks before. Then Georgia congressional representative John Lewis riveted us all.

If you don't know about Congressman Lewis, you should learn. He was one of our nation's greatest heroes.

John Lewis was born in 1940, the son of sharecroppers back when Alabama officially practiced racial segregation. But he bristled at the reality that most white Americans treated

Black Americans as second-class citizens, particularly in the South. So as a college student he helped organize sit-ins and other protests throughout the South. In 1961 he became one of the original thirteen Freedom Riders—Black and white, mostly college students—who courageously rode buses through the South to help integrate interstate bus terminals. In 1963, when he was just twenty-three, he helped organize and became the youngest speaker at the historic March on Washington for Jobs and Freedom. In 1965 he helped lead the Selma march on Bloody Sunday.

During the civil rights movement he also led protests against segregated schools, bathrooms, lunch counters, restaurants, water fountains, swimming pools, public parks, and more, across the South and many places in the North. Congressman Lewis survived numerous white mobs that tormented him. He recovered from multiple concussions. He was spat on, and had hot coffee poured on him and cigarettes snuffed out on his skin. But no matter what he experienced, he practiced nonviolence and love.[34]

With Carmen and Tamika at my side, I had the honor of introducing this civil rights icon and American hero.

"We were beaten, tear-gassed, trampled by horses. But we never gave up. We never gave in," he told the crowd about his experiences on Blood Sunday. "You must never, ever give up or give in. You must keep your faith, keep moving your feet, and keep putting your bodies on the line."

He encouraged us to get in trouble, "good trouble, necessary trouble," as he called the fight to make America a more humane and just society.

As the crowd roared, I got goose bumps.

By the end of that year, all three items in our justice package had been introduced in Congress, and the Juvenile Justice and Delinquency Prevention Act won enough votes to be reauthorized. We hadn't accomplished everything we had hoped for, but we had gotten closer to our goals. And like all the brave and stubbornly hopeful road warriors who had gone before us, we accepted Congressman John Lewis's charge to "continue to walk and work together, until we redeem the soul of America."

I was beginning to see how each experience in my life had prepared me for the next—from being the child of immigrants, to our family's visits to Palestine, to going to a high school where kids of color were over-policed, to my decision to wear a hijab, to getting married and becoming a mom, to supporting my community after 9/11, to standing up for the rights of Muslims, to being mentored by Basemah and even losing her, to standing up for my own children, to supporting Black Lives Matter, to expanding that vision to advocating for all people's rights.

The #March2Justice was the most powerful experience I had ever had in my life. But little did I know, it was preparing me for a bigger march that would touch far more people and make a much greater impact. Something bigger was happening, as I joined with Tamika and Carmen and other like-minded people who were called to serve all of humanity.

CHAPTER 21

My Name Is Linda Sarsour

I was lying across my bed, scrolling through Facebook two days after Donald Trump had gotten elected, when I saw an event page for a Million Women March scheduled to take place on the morning after Inauguration Day.

Trump had vilified Mexicans and directed hatred against women, Muslims, immigrants, disabled people, Gold Star families . . . The list of people Trump had offended went on and on. Now here was a march calling for all women to stand in unity and solidarity—Black women, Latina women, immigrant women, queer and trans women, and so on.

Hmm, why aren't Muslim women invited?

The fact that we hadn't been included really bothered me, especially since inciting fear against Muslims and banning Muslims from immigrating to the United States had been among the centerpieces of Donald Trump's hateful presidential campaign. But if I'm gonna be honest, even when Hillary Clinton had spoken of Muslims, she'd only done it when talking about keeping the nation safe from terrorists.

So I clicked on the event and left a comment: "This is a great endeavor. I hope you will also include Muslim women and Muslim communities."

I wrote it not realizing that my comment would go viral. Within a few hours it had thousands of likes. Then, the next thing I knew, Tamika was calling.

"I see you're commenting on the Women's March page," she said. "Why don't you come and help us organize?"

"I should have known you were already on board," I said.

"You know it!" she exclaimed.

"Well, if you're down, I'm down," I replied, knowing that Carmen would soon roll up her sleeves. By that time, whenever one of us was asked, all of us would get involved.

Now, this is where things start getting a little complicated. We had a lot of conversations behind the scenes, and the organizers agreed that Tamika, Carmen, and I would co-lead the March, along with Bob Bland, a young white woman in New York City who was a fashion designer and one of the people who had thought of the march. But it wasn't just us who headed up the planning. We dreamed that maybe we could get 250,000 people to show up. So amazing people like Janaye Ingram, a political organizer who lived in New Jersey, and filmmaker Paola Mendoza also worked behind the scenes, helping to secure permits, handle logistics, organize the program, and navigate the thousands of issues that had to be managed to pull off a march that size. On any given day more than forty women might be working at headquarters on the many parts of the campaign.

Carmen and I were charged with pulling together a diverse group of women—Jewish, African American, Asian, Latina, Muslim, Indigenous, queer, trans, and so on. This group would develop Unity Principles to join many diverse communities of people together and help everyone know that we weren't just marching against Trump. We were marching *for* something—the right for everyone to live freely, to practice their religion and experience justice no matter their race, religion, sexual orientation, gender, how much money they had, the nation they'd come from or been born in, and so on.

After that I worked with Paola to create the onstage program. But most of my time was spent raising money. What were some of the things we needed money for?

"We need money for security," one of the women said.

"We need money for the stage, tents, lights, a sound system, and Jumbotrons," said another.

"Don't forget internet hot spots so we can livestream!"

"And we want to be inclusive," another person added. "We need lifts so that disabled people can participate; sign language interpreters; medical and ambulance services."

"We need to pay our artists' and speakers' travel and hotel expenses."

As you can see, the list was long. Money, money, money—the pressure was on!

Perpetual anxiety

Now, I had done some meaningful things up until that point, but the organizing was still nerve-wracking. I felt overwhelmed by the list. Sometimes my heart raced. Other times my knees knocked. But each day I took at least one step forward in partnership as countless diverse women came together.

Organizing the Women's March became the most monumental undertaking of my life. For about three months I devoted every atom of my being to planning it.

"Already?" I would groan at six each morning when my alarm clock would go off. I'd just gone to bed at three a.m., but it was time to get up and go at it again. I was tempted to pull up the covers and put the pillow over my head, but this wasn't about me; it was about us.

Fortunately, my family had my back.

"I will take care of your children," Yumma had told me.

I would drag myself out of bed, lumber straight to the shower, and let the water cascade over my face. But I wasn't alone. All of the organizers sacrificed work time, family time, time off during the holiday season, and more in order to be in this movement 100 percent.

At times working with women of different races was challenging. For most of us who identify as Black or Brown, this kind of work wasn't new. But this was the first time that some of the white women were learning about and working on these types of causes. Some of them had grown accustomed to being in charge. Most had little experience working alongside and answering to Black and Brown women, particularly Tamika, who is petite but also a fireball. The Black and Brown women had far more experience in organizing protest movements. Also, many of the things that the white women were upset about were new issues to them but old to us.

"Look, we're with you," we told them. "But there are communities in this country who have been grappling with racism and misogyny for a long time. So we need to be clear that we're not just marching from a place of rage. We need to be proactive about demanding change."

We had a lot of very difficult but worthwhile conversations about race and racism in particular. Though often uncomfortable, engaging in these challenging conversations proved essential to our success.

My made-up mind

It was about a week before the inauguration when I turned on the TV in my hotel room. I was surprised to see an old man crying his eyes out.

I remember him saying he'd gotten the shock of his life when he'd opened his e-mail—just like Muhammad Ali had hit him in the stomach.

As I listened, Mr. Brotman explained that for sixty years he had officially announced the presidential inauguration that takes place after each American president's oath of office. The inauguration for John F. Kennedy? He was there. Lyndon B. Johnson, Richard Nixon, Gerald Ford, Jimmy Carter, Ronald Reagan, George Bush the father and George Bush the son, Bill Clinton, Barack Obama—you name the past eleven presidents, and Mr. Brotman had announced them as they'd walked in the presidential inauguration. It was something he looked forward to doing every four years. He'd planned for the 2017 inauguration to be the last before he retired. Two weeks before the event, Donald Trump fired him. Only a bully would do that to an elder on the verge of retirement.

Making a bad situation much worse, Mr. Brotman had just lost his wife. He said he had been so disappointed, he'd considered suicide!

Suicide?

WHOA! My heart dropped into my stomach.

Mr. Brotman answered, looking lost, When the host asked him what he was going to do, Mr. Brotman didn't know.

Well, he might not have known, but I had an idea. Because you know me. I was not going to allow this injustice to happen to this old man without attempting to address it.

"Look," I said when I walked into the office. "The way that this march is gonna start is Charlie Brotman is going to announce our march."

Everyone just stared at me.

"Who in the world is Charlie Brotman?"

"Charlie Brotman has announced every president since Eisenhower in the inauguration," I said. "Donald Trump just fired him."

You should have seen all the blank looks on the women's faces. They were looking at me like I was out of my mind.

"Uh, you came here to ask us permission for an old white guy to open our Women's March?"

"Yeah, that's what I'm saying."

"Uh, okay," they said. "If you find him, go get him."

I picked up the phone and tracked him down.

"How about if I tell you that you can announce something that is gonna be ten times the size of Trump's inauguration?" I asked him. "It will be the biggest event that you ever did in your entire life."

"Umm . . . ," he said, mainly because he probably didn't know who I was.

But I gave it one last shot. "Look, we're doing a Women's March, and it's gonna be big."

He wasn't on social media, so he didn't know who any of us were. I think it was the conviction in my voice that persuaded him.

"All right, I'm there," he told me.

From darkness to light

Before we got to the Women's March, we had to survive the inauguration.

Inauguration Day was tough. The mood in Washington was dark. Helicopters droned overhead, surveilling the scene. People in red MAGA hats were everywhere, brimming with pride that the man they'd voted for had won. Donald Trump made a divisive speech that focused on poverty, crime, gangs, and drugs. He pitted Americans against one another and America against the world.

Who divides people in an inauguration speech? Shouldn't speeches by a president bring people together? If ever there were a time to protest, it was now.

Women poured out of trains, climbed down from buses, and pulled up in cars. The protesters came sporting the pink knit hats with peaked ears that had become the signature look of our demonstration.

"Where are you from?" the women would ask as they saw each other.

"Chicago."

"Jackson, Mississippi."

"Tucson."

"The great state of Texas!"

"Miami in the house!"

My heart soared that so many women were coming to repudiate President Trump's division and hatred.

That night, while we were pulling together the final details, I noticed that my Twitter feed had become unusually active. When I stopped to check it out, I noticed that pictures of women wearing pink hats and T-shirts with our Women's March logo were already flying down my page. At first I was confused. It was the middle of the night; our march hadn't started yet. I also kept seeing the Shepard Fairey poster of the Bangladeshi Muslim woman wearing an American flag, Old Glory, as her hijab—the image that so many people wrongly thought was me. But then I started checking out the hashtags: #WomensMarchFrance, #WomensMarchNigeria, #WomensMarchNewZealand, #WomensMarchIndonesia, #WomensMarchSouthAfrica. Suddenly I was overcome with a sense of how big this event we'd been organizing might turn out to be.

"Hey, look at this," I said to one of the other women in our planning suite.

"I'm busy. What is it?"

"Just look!"

"Who are these women?"

"I don't know."

"Where is it?"

"Australia."

Then I'd walk over to the next organizer.

"You have to check this out. There's a Women's March happening in India."

Kenya, the Netherlands, London—long before daybreak in the US, women were marching all over the world!

By then about 222,000 people had RSVPed on Facebook, and another 251,000 indicated an interest. But that was just the Washington march. Organizers from around the country were staging sister events. In New York and LA, of course, but also Cleveland, Detroit, Chicago, Atlanta, Miami, Kansas City, Dallas, Houston, Phoenix, Las Vegas. The list went on and on.

We scrolled through social media all night watching march after march. It was a beautiful experience.

The most beautiful thing

As our ten a.m. start time drew near, the area backstage began to fill up—Washington DC's mayor, Muriel Bowser; LaDonna Harris, president of Americans for Indian Opportunity; LGBTQ+ and transgender activist Janet Mock; actress America Ferrera; May Ali, daughter of Muhammad Ali; civil rights scholar and icon Dr. Angela Davis; Sybrina Fulton, Lucia McBath, Maria Hamilton, and Gwen Carr, the mothers of four Black Americans who had been killed by police or white vigilante violence; musical artists and activists such as Janelle Monáe; actress Scarlett Johansson; and many, many more. We were very proud to have curated a lineup that represented all of America.

My cell began to ring.

"Charlie Brotman's here!"

"I'll be right there!" I said, and rushed over to greet him. "Mr. Brotman! Thank you so much for coming. I'm Linda Sarsour, the woman who called you."

"Linda! Nice to meet you," he said. "This is quite an event!"

"Didn't I tell you that it would be big?"

"You sure did!"

Before long it was time to announce the march.

"You ready, sir?" I asked.

"I sure am!"

"Well, let's go!"

I walked Mr. Brotman up the steps and onto the stage. What I saw when I reached the top just took my breath away—an endless sea of pink humanity. To the left of the stage the people just went on and on and on. Stage right, same thing: boundless people. There were people straight ahead for as far as I could see. People crammed all down the side streets; there were even people behind the stage! An ocean of baby-pink, rose, salmon, fuchsia, blush, and hot-pink signs and hats and jackets!

I wish you could have seen the pure joy on Mr. Brotman's face.

"This is the most beautiful thing I have ever witnessed in my life," he said as he burst into tears.

"It *is* beautiful, isn't it?"

As far as I could see was a rolling crowd, all the shades of pink, an infinity of faces. I felt the power of their energy, *our* energy. Together!

No apologies

The program began with an Indigenous service. We wanted Native Americans to appear on the program first to give honor to them and to remind people of the fact that they are the original inhabitants of this land.

Then a wonderful lineup of young people, queer people, Muslims, immigrants, all spoke, followed by the introduction of the four event chairs: Bob, Carmen, Tamika, and me. My mom, my kids, my sister and her kids, and my movement family joined me as we were officially introduced to the world as the co-chairs of the Women's March.

I stood between Tamika on one side and Carmen on the other—my sisters in the movement.

The social justice Voltron was in action on our largest stage.

I knew that that was a great moment for my community. We were being livestreamed in more than eighty countries. We were on MSNBC, CNN, *Democracy Now!*, everywhere!

It was in this moment that I realized something incredible: I was the Muslim American with the biggest platform on the planet—not just in the US, but in the world! I didn't know it at the time, but more than 3.5 million people, mostly women, were hitting the streets—in New York, in Los Angeles, in Houston, in Chicago, in New Orleans, in Little Rock, in Salt Lake City, and in smaller cities and towns everywhere!

I took a deep breath and centered myself. This was a moment of great responsibility.

Here is what I said to myself: *This is your opportunity to reintroduce Muslims to the American public. To reintroduce us not as terrorists or "others" but as fellow Americans and people who are deeply committed to racial justice, to economic justice. To send the message that we are all in this struggle together. To let people know that when you see me and my mom and my children, we are in this with you—and to say you will not be free unless I am free and my family is free.*

But here's a big difference between me and my Voltron sisters. Bob, Carmen, and Tamika—they had their speeches written down and they read them off paper. You already know, I do not write things down. I just say whatever I gotta say—whatever moves me in that moment.

I strode to the front of the stage along with Yumma, Sabreen, Tamir, and Sajida. I could barely contain my wonder as I looked out upon the endless sea of pink hats and hijabs and homemade signs. I took a deep breath and inhaled the beauty of the WE THE PEOPLE signs of Brown and Black women that Amplifier Art had so beautifully rendered.

Then I opened my mouth.

"Assalamu alaikum! May peace be upon you, brothers and sisters." It was strange listening to the way my voice echoed down the mall. "My name is Linda Sarsour, and I am one of the national co-chairs for the Women's March on Washington. I stand here before you, unapologetically Muslim American, unapologetically Palestinian American, unapologetically from Brooklyn, New York."

The crowd went wild! I felt goose bumps rise all over my body. My voice was powerful and strong.

"Sisters and brothers, you are what democracy looks like. Sisters and brothers, you are my hope for my community.

"I will respect the presidency, but I will not respect this president of the United States of America. I will not respect an administration that won an election on the backs of Muslims and Black people and undocumented people and Mexicans and people with disabilities, and on the backs of women.

"Many of our communities—including my community, the Muslim community—have been suffering in silence for the past fifteen years under the Bush administration and under the Obama administration. The very things that you are outraged by during this election season—the Muslim registry program, the banning of the Muslims, the dehumanization of the community that I come from—that has been our reality for the past fifteen years.

"Sisters and brothers, if you have come here today as your first time at a march, I welcome you. I ask you to stand and continue to keep your voices loud for Black women, for Native women, for undocumented women, for our LGBTQ+ communities, for people with disabilities.

"You can count on me, your Palestinian Muslim sister, to keep her voice loud, keep her feet on the streets, keep my head held high because I am not afraid.

"Sisters and brothers, fear is a choice. We are the majority. We are the conscience of these United States of America. We are this nation's moral compass. If you want to know if you are going the right way, follow women of color, sisters and brothers. We know where we need to go, and we know where justice is, because when we fight for justice, we fight for it for all people, for all our communities.

"I want to remind you that the reason why you are here today is because mothers and yoga teachers and organizers and bakers came out to organize. Ordinary people made this happen. No corporate dollars, no money from corporations. This is your dollars. This is your work. You made this happen.

"I am honored to stand here today on the stage as a national co-chair with Tamika and Carmen, who are my sisters, but also with my family, because I organize for my mother. I march for my daughters and all my children. But most of all I am my Palestinian-grandmother-who-lived-in-occupied-territory's wildest dreams, sisters and brothers, and I'm so proud to be here with all of you.

"Justice for all."

The crowd roared as I moved to the back of the stage and the next speakers stepped forward.

And in a moment it all was over. I looked up and saw my kids and my mom. She was crying. Once I saw Yumma cry, my chest and my throat tightened. Then all of the emotions I had suppressed over the previous nine weeks came rushing up. I started bawling—not tears of pain or shame but tears of pride and joy and relief.

We had done it!

For nine grueling weeks, women of all colors and creeds—women who until that moment had not known one another—had come together to birth a global movement for change.

Bob, Carmen, Tamika, and I had been the face of the movement. But as three women of color, Carmen, Tamika, and I had taken a tremendous responsibility upon our shoulders. We knew that if the march succeeded, it would be a success for Indigenous women, Black women, Chicana, Latina, Asian, Muslim women, all women of color.

And we had created something that was not just successful but something uniquely and indescribably beautiful!

We had put the forces of hate and division on notice that, no matter whether they valued us or not, we were centering our own people, and their moment of reckoning was here. We would bring our sisters, mothers, daughters, grandmothers, and aunts. We would bring along the men who were our allies. Together we would change the world.

And we were in it together!

We had done it

I knew I had made my community proud. I had dignified the lives of my parents—hardworking immigrants who had come to this country in search of a better life, and my father in particular, who had worked sixteen-hour days for thirty-five years.

So I wept with relief, with pride, and with joy.

As the tears streamed down my face and I tasted their saltiness on my lips, I also thought about my mom, who had successfully raised seven children in this country, though English wasn't her first language and she didn't understand American schools.

"Look, you did it! You did everything you could," I said, holding her by the shoulders and looking deeply into her glassy eyes. My mind flashed back to nights at the kitchen table, when she'd tried to help us with our homework but couldn't because of the language barrier or because she hadn't received much education herself. I remembered the times when I'd humbly stepped in to help my younger brothers and sisters. I thought of all the evenings when I'd translated paperwork and filled out forms and applications for her. I thought of all the times when the look in her eyes had said everything—that she felt embarrassed, or inadequate, or that what she was doing was just not enough for us.

"Look where it got me! Look where it got us!" I exclaimed to her. She just bawled and fell limp in my arms. When I saw Yumma weep, every fiber of my being wanted to comfort her. "There is nothing that you could have done better!" I sobbed.

I also flashed back to moments when I'd overcome my own uncertainty and fear, and connected with my own inner courage so I could take charge, be extra responsible, help my siblings and family in the areas where my parents could not. The long and the short of it was, they had been visionary and courageous enough to come to this exciting, frightening, new, and overwhelming country in search of their American dream.

She had done it; my father had done it; I had done it; we had done it!

The next day Yumma handed me the phone.

It was my grandmother. She too was bawling her eyes out. I hadn't known it, but this amazing woman born in 1927 had been watching me on livestream from El Bireh.

For a woman who had lost her land, and lived under an occupation, and seen trauma and pain, death and sorrow, seeing her Palestinian granddaughter standing on a stage in front of more than one million people and broadcast all over the world—saying, "I am unapologetically Palestinian" and "I am my Palestinian grandmother's wildest dream manifested"— meant more to her than I can ever know.

Suddenly her granddaughter was humanizing Palestinians to the entire world, people who had long been unseen, unheard, vilified, and talked about. I was glad to have given this gift to all of my family living under occupation. Even though I'm in the US, I'm still fighting for them.

Later we would learn that another 4.6 million Americans across the nation,[35] and 6 million people around the world had joined the half million[36] of us who had come to Washington to march for our collective freedom that day. That made 7 million people total, transforming the murk and gloom of Inauguration Day into a movement for change that was hopeful, sustaining, and bright like the gleaming white dome on top of the US Capitol.

Ours was likely the largest single-day demonstration in US history.[37]

Our brilliance and resolve had inspired the entire world, and in the light and likeness of so many women, a new resistance had been born.

CHAPTER 22

What I'm Doing Now

In April 2018, just one block from the corner in Crown Heights where I had once worked in my father's bodega, a young Black man, Saheed Vassell, was fatally shot by police. He had been holding a metal pipe when police approached him. The neighbors all knew that he had bipolar disorder—a mental illness—and was harmless. No one was afraid of him. He did odd jobs for the barbershop on the block, sweeping and taking out the trash. When he died, Saheed was thirty-four, close to my age, which meant we would have passed each other often in the neighborhood.

When Yaba heard the news about Saheed, his usually playful demeanor grew somber.

"He must have come into my store," he reflected, wiping a large hand down his suddenly weary face. Yaba thought he remembered the man's parents, hardworking Jamaican immigrants.

There's a protest for Saheed tonight, my father messaged me the next evening.

I'll be there, I typed.

I was at the Justice League NYC office with Carmen and Tamika at the time. When I told them where I was going, they both said they were coming too.

That evening, on the corner of Montgomery and Utica, hundreds of my Brooklyn neighbors poured into the street in front of the two-story red-and-gold brick buildings, where Crown Cleaners, the bright red awning of Chucky Fresh Market, and the bright yellow storefront of Troy Deli, now occupied the storefront my father once owned.

Black mothers and fathers arrived pushing their toddlers in strollers; college students rolled up in their Black Lives Matter T-shirts; middle-aged people showed up wearing suits and work uniforms; community elders came expressing sorrow and disgust. A community organizer wandered around carrying clipboards in hand, registering people to vote.

"Mental illness should never be a death sentence!" some of the protesters chanted, while others yelled "Murder!" again and again. Their voices reverberated in the intersection before rising like a prayer into the evening sky.

Several speakers shouted into bullhorns that the police could easily have subdued Saheed without killing him. When Saheed's mom stepped to the mike, a hush fell over the crowd.

"My son was a good young man," I recall her saying, her voice sounding anguished. "I want to make sure people know he was good."

That's when it began.

A Black man wearing a T-shirt and long dreadlocks walked up to me with a quizzical look on his face.

"Aren't you Nick's daughter?"

"Hi, yes, I'm Linda."

"I used to see you in his store. . . ."

"Oh yeah, I worked behind the cash register."

"Oh snap! I thought you looked familiar," another man said, flashing a wide smile. "I don't know if you remember me, but I used to come in after school and buy a pack of apple Now and Later candies and an orange drink."

"Of course I remember you," I laughed, seeing reflected in his adult face the charming smile of the teen boy sporting the hi-top fade and brightly colored 8-ball jacket.

Again and again it happened—grown men enfolding me in bear hugs.

"Thanks for coming back for Saheed," they told me.

"I wouldn't miss it," I answered.

"How's Nick?"

"He's well," I replied. "In fact he told me about the protest. He knew I would want to come."

"Tell him I said hello."

These men had once been boys whose names Yaba knew, whose parents he'd asked about as he'd folded down the tops of brown paper bags in his precise, punctuated way.

One of these men could be Jerome, I reflected, recalling the hungry boy who had shoplifted and whom my father had met not with punishment but with kindness, and the belief that he would do better next time.

No wonder I am an activist, I thought with a sudden

sense of surprise, goose bumps rising all over my body.

I hadn't known it then, but my life had been training me—by speaking Arabic with Yumma, helping my father at the store, walking the streets of El Bireh, on debate team at John Jay, working with desperate women who came to AAANY looking for help in the years after 9/11, and, of course, in both loving and losing Basemah.

Now, standing a block from the place where Linda Sarsour's Spanish & American Food Center had once served the neighborhood for thirty-five years, wonderful memories flooded over me.

I hardly noticed when someone handed me a megaphone, but as I lifted it to my lips, I felt the pain of Saheed's loss, and the conviction that he'd deserved better, that we all deserved better.

"Saheed was one of us!" I shouted into the crowd. "We will fight so that what happened to our brother Saheed will not happen to anyone else!"

Then I handed the megaphone to the next person, my eyes searching for Carmen and Tamika on the crowded street. That's when I saw both women, eyes bright in the twilight, raising their fists in the air, chanting, "Justice for Saheed!"

When the streetlights came on, they illuminated the faces of people I had grown up with in my beloved Brooklyn, and they illuminated the two women by my side as we marched down Utica Avenue, the traffic slowing behind us.

As I stood beside my sisters amid the roar of voices, my own fist pumping, no one but God heard me whisper: "This is where I belong."

Daring to dream

I wish I could tell you that the march for Saheed was the last one I walked in, but that would ignore the reality of life for Black and Brown people and immigrants in the United States.

Today my life is all about standing up—keeping my voice loud and showing up for social justice causes that might need a hopeful spirit and tireless feet. Because injustice continues to occur, particularly in those communities.

I also found myself in Washington, participating in an act of civil disobedience on behalf of undocumented people. We were protesting the Trump administration's call to end the Deferred Action for Childhood Arrivals (DACA) program that former president Barack Obama had established to protect more than 650,000 undocumented immigrants, nicknamed "Dreamers," whose parents had brought them to the United States—mainly from Mexico, El Salvador, Guatemala, and Honduras—when they were just children.[38] Today most are adults. Many have only lived in the United States, and lots of those born someplace else have only vague memories of that place.

We call these young adults "Dreamers" because they see themselves as Americans and are pursuing the American dream. Countless numbers are enrolled in or have completed college. They are baristas, and web designers, and grocery store clerks, and sales representatives, and electrical engineers, and cell phone store managers, and grad students. They are earning a living for themselves, their kids, and their families—and they are shaping the future of our great nation. But the Trump administration wanted to send them back to countries they've never lived in, with streets they may have never walked and languages they may not even speak.

Demonstrations took place all over the country.

So that day I walked through the Capitol, the sound of our voices and the heels of our shoes echoing in the granite halls.

Also in the Capitol that day, Muslim and Jewish leaders gathered from across the country, joining with the immigrant rights groups and undocumented people, many from Central America.

But among all the people I saw in the Capitol, I will never forget the moment I saw her. A little Mexican girl, maybe six years old. She was wearing colorful butterfly wings.

Butterflies.

With just a flap of their wings, these beautiful insects can fly over borders and soar unfettered. They symbolize free-dom for undocumented people.

Turquoise blue, canary yellow, fuchsia, and chartreuse, this little girl's butterfly wings were almost as large as she was.

I watched her approach an imam whom she had heard speaking Spanish.

"Quiero volar como una mariposa"—I want to fly like a butterfly—she said, gazing into the tan bearded face and kind eyes of this Texas-born convert to Islam.

Another imam overheard her request and smiled down at the child from his six-foot-five height. He, in turn, called over a second imam, also a towering man. Together the two spiritual leaders lifted the child high above their heads.

"I'm flying!" she laughed, her voice sparkling with glee.

Everyone clapped and cheered, and the child's mother put one hand over her heart and dabbed her teary eyes with the other.

I pulled out my cell phone and took her picture. I keep it with me because moments like these sustain me. Human exchanges full of love and optimism armored and helped me confront the Trump administration's many atrocities. Unspeakable acts like ripping children from the arms of parents seeking asylum at the southern border.

America is a nation of people seeking refuge.

Raising the torch of freedom above her head, the statue of Lady Liberty stands in New York Harbor, awash in a beautiful blue green. In the museum at its base, you can find Emma Lazarus's poem "The New Colossus."

> *Give me your tired, your poor,*
> *Your huddled masses yearning to breathe free,*
> *The wretched refuse of your teeming shore.*
> *Send these, the homeless, tempest-tost to me,*
> *I lift my lamp beside the golden door!*[39]

That is America's promise.

Yet the Trump administration locked an untold number of innocent children in cages for months, even years, and deported their parents without them. On those days when I am plagued with questions about whether to keep going with the work I do, my memories of the little Mexican American girl with butterfly wings flying joyfully above the two imams strengthen me, especially when it feels like my own life is at risk.

Though President Biden is now in office, we know that we must continue to push forward so that undocumented people of all ages experience all of the American dream.

Stand with the Dreamers

The "American dream" is the belief that anyone can achieve their goals and have a great life if they work hard and stay on the right path. Many people move—or immigrate—to America for this promise of a better life.

"Dreamer" is the nickname that we use for children who moved to the United States with their families. Some Dreamers are brought to America as young as infants. They usually have no memory of the country they were born in. They are raised in America, go to school in America, and get jobs in America. They set goals, work hard, and chase the American dream.

Many Dreamers live with the fear that they may be deported (kicked out by the government) just because they weren't born in America. It's unfair, and nobody should have to live with that fear.

When we stand with the Dreamers, we are fighting for our immigrant brothers' and sisters' right to live and work and chase their dreams in the country that they call home.

Say her name

In May 2020, I was invited to Louisville, Kentucky, to meet the family of Breonna Taylor and help work on her police brutality case.

Breonna was a brilliant twenty-six-year-old Black woman with bright eyes and a gleaming smile who helped the people of Louisville as an emergency medical technician. Even in the middle of the COVID-19 pandemic, she worked helping sick people in the hospital. Her mom loved her; her sister loved her; her aunties loved her; her friends loved her; her community loved her. So did her boyfriend, Kenneth Walker.

Shortly after midnight on March 13, Breonna and Kenneth were resting in bed, watching TV. Suddenly there was pounding on the door.

Kenneth asked who it was, wondering what would make someone pound on their door at midnight.

He and Breonna didn't hear an answer, but the pounding continued. Needless to say, they felt fearful. Kenneth drew the firearm he is licensed to carry. Suddenly the door flew off its hinges and men rushed in. Kenneth fired toward the door.

But because it was nighttime and the police hadn't announced themselves, Kenneth didn't know that he'd shot at the police. They had burst into Breonna and Kenneth's home with what is called a no-knock warrant—one that allows them just to knock down the door—looking for a drug dealer who didn't even live there.

The police then unloaded a hail of bullets. Six hit Breonna, killing her as she stood in the hallway awakened by the loud noises.

It is sickening. Worse, the officers never found drugs in her apartment.

Needless to say, no innocent and unarmed person should be gunned down by the police in the sanctity of their home.

So we—Tamika D. Mallory, Mysonne Linen, Angelo Pinto, and myself—traveled to Louisville to create a campaign to help her get justice. We led a series of rallies and direct actions, including one in the attorney general's front yard and another on what would have been Breonna's twenty-seventh birthday. People such as Beyoncé, Cardi B, Lizzo, Ariana Grande, John Legend, Meek Mill, Jordan Peele, Megan Thee Stallion, Jada Pinkett Smith, and Willow Smith tweeted in support.

We marched, blocked streets, and engaged in civil disobedience, a strategy where you intentionally and nonviolently break the law with the hope that your action will help change a law or policy.

On the day we protested peacefully in the attorney general's front yard, almost ninety of us got arrested as a form of civil disobedience. A number of celebrities joined and got arrested with us, including Houston Texans wide receiver Kenny Stills, hip-hop artists Trae tha Truth and YBN Cordae, and reality show stars Yandy Smith and Porsha Williams—the granddaughter of the famous civil rights activist Rev. Hosea Williams, who'd helped lead the Bloody Sunday march that Mr. B. had taught us about.[40][41]

Eventually public pressure caused three police officers to be fired, one because he'd discharged ten shots blindly through the wall and window of the apartment. But as I write this book, none of the police officers have been charged with Breonna's murder. How can a woman be killed in her own home and no one be held accountable?

I'm a human being

While we were in Louisville, we got a call from Indianapolis, where we drove to meet the family of a nineteen-year-old Black man named McHale Rose. Rose had been shot by the Indianapolis police in April. He was one of three people the Indianapolis police killed in literally a twenty-four-hour period. But none of the officers were being held accountable. One of the people killed, twenty-one-year-old Dreasjon Reed livestreamed his murder on Facebook with his phone. Shortly after that an off-duty officer hit a pregnant Black woman as she walked along the side of the road.

Adding insult to injury, shortly thereafter a cop named Derek Chauvin murdered a man named George Floyd. So we got into our car and drove for nine hours to Minneapolis.

George Floyd was an African American man whom the police arrested as he sat in his car. He had just shopped in a corner store and used a twenty-dollar bill the cashier believed might be fake. Four police showed up and two pulled their guns on Floyd, who was cooperating and repeatedly begging them not to shoot him. As he was complying, the officers took him down to the ground next to the police cruiser. Three other police officers failed to intervene as Officer Chauvin knelt on Mr. Floyd's neck for nine minutes and twenty-nine seconds, killing him.

"I can't breathe," he cried out more than twenty times.[42]

As community members begged Officer Chauvin to stop, a seventeen-year-old girl, Darnella Frazier, caught the entire incident on video and posted it to Facebook, and the outraged community caused it to go viral.

By the time we arrived, the public outpouring of grief and anger had begun. Protests were already in full swing—and it was the most remarkable thing I've ever seen in my life. I'm accustomed to watching young people engaged in uprisings risk their lives because they want freedom. Now on the streets of Minneapolis I witnessed the very same thing: Black people rising up and saying, "Our lives matter!"

On poster board, on manila folders, on the inside of cardboard boxes, little children, community elders, college students, and parents had created beautiful paintings and drawings of Mr. Floyd's face. They hoisted sign after sign to the sky that read: BLACK LIVES MATTER; STOP KILLING US; SILENCE = CONSENT; MY SKIN COLOR IS NOT A CRIME.

My skin vibrated with the energy of the thousands of people who turned out to protest. I witnessed an ocean of signs and every shade of skin and hair, shape of body, style of clothing and tattoo, and colors of humanity. Transfixed, at one point I even stopped walking.

"Sorry, I didn't mean to run into you, sis," a woman said after she ran into me, as the sea of humanity streamed past me.

"No worries," I told her, suddenly returning to my senses.

The river of people was as beautiful as the butterfly girl taking flight.

Minneapolis is home to a large community of immigrants from Somalia, who had come to the United States fleeing a civil war. One night I watched a group of six girls dressed in long conservative dresses with black hijabs and matching face masks to protect themselves against the coronavirus. I chuckled as they rolled up the hems of their dresses and tuck them into the pants they were wearing underneath. I silently cheered them as they protested in front of police wearing helmets, bulletproof vests, and military boots, and carrying clear plexiglass shields. The girls were claiming their America.

Suddenly the police started shooting tear gas into the crowd. People screamed, and they started coughing and choking, even turning and running.

Then the most incredible thing happened.

As the police shot tear gas and the crowd began to disperse, I witnessed these Somali girls run toward the canisters as the containers would land. They would pick up the canister, cock their arm, and throw it back toward the police.

At one point, as I covered my face and retreated from the smoke, I watched them throw ten canisters back in a row.

Swish, swish, swish, swish.

"Whaaaat?"

"Would you look at this?" people exclaimed.

The cops were astonished. Suddenly they retreated. Within moments there were no more cops around—they'd disappeared.

I wish you could have heard the sound of the crowd welling up. Everyone started cheering. It was crazy!

I was astounded as well. With my shirt pulled up over my face, I made my way to them.

"How can you pick them up with your bare hands—aren't they hot?" I asked.

"No, they're just a little warm," they told me, their eyes gleaming between their hijabs and their face masks.

They had already survived a civil war and military violence. Now they found themselves using skills learned during a war to protect themselves in the place that had been sold as the land of the free. Yet they stood their ground, owning their right to peacefully protest.

Allies and agitators

During the days and weeks that followed, it was also exciting to see so many white allies joining alongside Black and Brown people. The crowds swelled to an enormous size.

But I witnessed different categories of white folks. There were a handful of white allies who got it, knew what they were doing, and were willing to put their bodies on the line to keep the cops from abusing Black people.

"What can I do to support you?" they asked.

"Thank you for coming," I heard one Black organizer say. "One thing you can do is put your bodies between us and the police. We already know the police will hurt us, but they are more likely to listen to and less likely to harm you."

There were also white people who thought these protests

to save Black lives were a spectator sport they attended to watch for entertainment.

Then there was a third category of white people: *provocateurs*.

People who came out to agitate, to provoke trouble, often by breaking windows, destroying property, spray-painting buildings, or looting. People whose actions could move the media narrative away from the story of people peacefully protesting a police killing of an unarmed Black person, and change it to a narrative of Black people looting and destroying property.

At one point I looked across an intersection and saw a white guy in his early twenties. He picked up a barricade, lifted it over his head, and slammed it to the ground, causing a leg of the barricade to break.

Why was he over there all by himself?

Suddenly it dawned on me what was happening. I walked up behind him.

"What are you doing?" I asked as he picked up another barricade. By now I knew that if young Black and Brown kids joined in, the media would change their narrative from one about a righteous protest to one about Black people as dangerous rioters; the agitators would win.

He just looked at me. "Really?" he said, then shook his head and slammed the barrier.

"Don't try to act like you're more angry than the Black people," I scolded, well aware that a small number of saboteurs want Black young people to think, *This white kid's doing it? I'm gonna do it too.*

The white guy's eyes widened.

"I've been doing this long enough to know that you're on somebody's payroll," I said. "We're not gonna play that here. So don't think these people don't know who you are and what you're doing. It's better for you to just put that barricade down and walk away. I won't tell anyone here that I know who you are."

"Fine," he said, and put the barricade down very slowly. Then he backed up and moved off.

Don't mess with Brooklyn!

"Yo, where do you know him from?" several young people asked.

"I don't know him from a hole in the wall," I told them. "But anytime you see that kind of behavior coming from a white person, know that that person isn't with you. These are not white bodies on the ground."

In other words, don't come to a protest pretending that you're supporting people, then do things that harm and make life even more difficult for them.

When we are allies to one another, it's important to behave respectfully, listen to what people need, and support them in the way they tell us they need to be supported. We don't create additional problems by pursuing our own agenda and disregarding theirs.

One step forward

In the days and weeks afterward, something spectacular happened—something that I hope you had the chance to be a part of. In Minneapolis and across the nation, much of America suddenly "got it," as hundreds of thousands of new racial-justice allies poured into the streets to participate in Black Lives Matter marches. Sadly, from the Twin Cities to New York City, from Portland to Philadelphia, and places in between, tens of thousands of Americans exercising their right to free speech and to peacefully protest encountered police in armored vehicles, wielding military weapons, and firing tear gas and rubber bullets. But for the first time many white people experienced firsthand a bit of the violence Black and Brown people and immigrants experience regularly at the hands of the police. And that has been a good thing. Shocked by how they were treated, many joined the conversation about the importance of social and racial justice and reforming policing.

Then in April 2021, after hearing a parade of witnesses, police, and forensic and legal experts—including the Minneapolis chief of police and Darnella Frazier, who'd filmed Mr. Floyd being killed—a jury consisting of twelve of his peers found Derek Chauvin guilty, on three counts, of killing George Floyd. The case was one of the first in the nation where a white police officer was held accountable for killing a Black person.

No, this verdict doesn't solve the deeper problems. But it is one step forward—an important step forward—toward improving our criminal justice system and creating the fair world that we all deserve, a world that cherishes all human life. Tragedies like climate change and the coronavirus epidemic are showing many of us how closely we are all intertwined. We can create the world in which justice prevails and every human being is valued, if we take action to see one another as fully human, join our arms, stand side by side, and all be in this together.

Ten Protests That Have Shaped America

Unlike in many nations around the world where it's illegal to stand up against the government, the United States Constitution guarantees Americans the right to make our voices heard when we disagree—by protesting. Here is a list of protests that have helped to shape our society. Whether Black Lives Matter or the Women's March, maybe you've been involved in some of them!

George Floyd/Black Lives Matter protests—May 26, 2020–present

Between fifteen and twenty-six million protesters marched in all fifty US states plus people took to the streets in over sixty countries worldwide to call for an end to systemic racism that has killed innocent Black people such George Floyd, Breonna Taylor, and Ahmaud Arbery. A main goal of these protests is to change the way that law enforcement takes place so that the police stop being violent toward and killing innocent Black people. Instead we want the government to put more money into programs that will help schools that serve low-income people and communities, and spend less money on the police.

March for Our Lives—March 24, 2018

Led by students, this protest drew as many as 800,000 people in Washington, DC, and marches took place all across the United States. Protesters were saddened and outraged at recent school shootings and marched for stricter gun laws so that kids would be safe at school.

March for Science—April 22, 2017
Over a million protesters around the world marched on Earth Day to push for governments to focus on climate change and how we can continue to live on this earth without destroying it. This came after President Trump refused to accept that climate change is a real issue.

Women's March on Washington—January 21, 2017
In the largest single-day protest in US history, about 500 thousand people gathered in Washington, DC, to march for women's rights, and between 3.2 and 5.2 million nationwide.[43] There were protests in eighty-one different countries and on every continent, including Antarctica. Another Women's March took place in 2018, this time with 1.5 million people, still making it into the top five biggest US protests.

Protests against Iraq War—February 15, 2003
At least half a million people in America, and between twelve and fourteen million people worldwide,[44] protested against President Bush's decision to invade Iraq.

Protesters called for the end to a war that was altogether unnecessary and killed many innocent people.

Million Man March—October 16, 1995
Somewhere between half a million and a million people (mostly Black men) gathered in front of the Capitol building in Washington, DC, to unite the Black community and to help get Black men registered to vote. Speeches were given by significant Black public figures such as Rosa Parks, Jesse Jackson, Maya Angelou, and Cornel West.

March on Washington for Lesbian, Gay, and Bi Equal Rights and Liberation—April 25, 1993
An estimated one million people gathered at the National Mall to demand a civil rights bill to end discrimination against lesbian, gay, and bisexual people. They also marched for reproductive rights and more funding for AIDS research, a disease that significantly impacted the LGBTQ+ community at the time.

Moratorium Against the Vietnam War—November 15, 1969
Over half a million Americans gathered in Washington, DC, to protest against the war in Vietnam, a war that most Americans didn't agree with. Protesters called for the US military to withdraw from Vietnam, yet another

war that seemed unnecessary and killed many innocent people.

March on Washington for Jobs and Freedom—August 28, 1963

Led by Dr. Martin Luther King Jr, this civil rights march brought a quarter of a million people to the National Mall. This is where Dr. King gave his famous "I Have a Dream" speech. The following year the Civil Rights Act of 1964 was enacted, making it illegal to discriminate based on race, color, sex, religion, or national origin (the country you were born in).

Women's Suffrage Procession—March 3, 1913

Over five thousand women gathered in Washington, DC, and marched for the right to vote, and a quarter million people came to watch. Despite their efforts, women weren't given the right to vote until 1920.

Acknowledgments

This book is a gift to all the young people all over the world who have blessed me with their stories, dreams and aspirations. I want to thank my own children, Tamir, Sabreen, and Sajida, for their understanding and patience throughout their lives as I spent so much time away from home working to build a more fair and just country that embraced them for all that they are. Although we are far from that country, they have inspired me to forge forward, knowing that only when we fight for what we deserve will we win. Thank you to all the Muslim Student Association (MSA) members and Students for Justice in Palestine organizers for reaffirming that the future of our community is bright. To all the undocumented youth who have risked their lives over the last decade, thank you for teaching me to be brave. To Black young people on the streets of Brooklyn and Louisville, thank you for your courage, your testimony, and for reminding me to "keep going." To Palestinian youth living in Palestine, thank you for your resilience, tenacity, and joyful spirits.

This book was a long time coming. I may not be able to visit every school or meet every student in the United States. This book was my way of connecting and teaching as many as I can. Everything I do is to uplift, motivate, and inspire you, and so I thank Hilary Beard for helping me birth this work. I'm also grateful for the incredible support from my editor, Deeba Zargarpur at Salaam Reads and the wonderful team at Simon & Schuster.

Special thanks to my family, best friends, and my movement families at Until Freedom and MPower Change for being my armor and my sanctuary in a dark and scary world. I couldn't do this work without you.

Glossary of Islamic and Arabic Terms

Allah (AH-lah)—the Arabic word for "God"

hajj (HAHJ)—the pilgrimage that Muslims make to Mecca

hijab (hee-JAHB)—a head covering worn by some Muslim women

imam (ee-MAHM)—the person who leads prayer in a mosque

Islam (is-LAHM)—one of the Abrahamic faiths; the word "Islam" comes from an Arabic word meaning "submission"

jihad (jee-HAHD)—the hard work of becoming a better person

Mecca (MEH-kuh)—a sacred Islamic city, located in Saudi Arabia

mosque (MAHSK)—the place where Muslims go to pray

Muslim (MUS-luhm)—someone who practices Islam

Qur'an (kuh-RAHN)—Islam's holy book

Ramadan (RAH-muh-dahn)—the month-long period when Muslims worship and do not eat or drink during daylight hours

salat (suh-LAHT)—the prayer Muslims complete five times each day

Endnotes

1 Huda. "The World's Muslim Population: Statistics and Key Facts" Learn Religions. Updated on October 24, 2018. https://www.learnreligions.com/worlds-muslim-population-2004480

2 Why Islam Editors. "What are the Pillars of Islam?" Why Islam. Accessed July 2021. https://www.whyislam.org/faqs/pillars/

3 History.com Editors. "State of Israel proclaimed." This Day in History: May 14, 1948. https://www.history.com/this-day-in-history/state-of-israel-proclaimed

4 Linda Sarsour. *We Are Not Here to Be Bystanders: A Memoir of Love and Resistance.* (Simon & Schuster, 2020), 31.

5 "Refugees." Holocaust Encyclopedia. Accessed July 2021. https://encyclopedia.ushmm.org/content/en/article/refugees

6 Lynette Holloway. "Reinventing John Jay High Amid Charges of Exclusion." *New York Times.* July 4, 2001. https://www.nytimes.com/2001/07/04/nyregion/reinventing-john-jay-high-amid-charges-of-exclusion.html?scp=1&sq=John+Jay+High+School+Brooklyn&st=nyt

7 History.com Editors. "September 11 Attacks." A&E Television Networks. Updated on September 22, 2021. www.history.com/topics/21st-century/9-11-attacks

8 Sarsour, 61.

9 ACLU Editors. "National Security Entry-Exit Registration System." Immigrants' Rights. Accessed July 2021. https://www.aclu.org/issues/immigrants-rights/immigrants-rights-and-detention/national-security-entry-exit-registration

10 U.S. Citizenship and Immigration Services Editors. "Glossary." Accessed July 2021. https://www.uscis.gov/tools/glossary

11 NYC.gov Editors. "Impact of Hurricane Sandy." NYC Community Development Disaster Recovery. Accessed July 2021. https://www1.nyc.gov/site/cdbgdr/about/About%20Hurricane%20Sandy.page#:~:text=Impact%20of%20Hurricane%20Sandy&text=The%20storm%20resulted%20in%20the,New%20Yorkers%20were%20temporarily%20displaced

12 Samantha Laine. "Why NYC students will be getting Islamic holidays off this year." *Christian Science Monitor*. March 4, 2015. https://www.csmonitor.com/USA/USA-Update/2015/0304/Why-NYC-students-will-be-getting-Islamic-holidays-off-this-year

13 Coalition for Muslim School Holidays Editors. "About Us." Accessed July 2021. http://eidinnyc.org/about-us/

14 Kirk Semple. "Council Votes for Two Muslim School Holidays." *New York Times*. June 30, 2009. https://www.nytimes.com/2009/07/01/nyregion/01muslim.html

15 Samantha Laine. "Islamic Holidays."

16 Sarsour, 128.

17 Sarsour, 134.

18 Taahira Thompson. "NYPD's Infamous Stop-and-Frisk Policy Found Unconstitutional." The Leadership Conference Education Fund. August 21, 2013. https://civilrights.org/edfund/resource /nypds-infamous-stop-and-frisk-policy-found-unconstitutional/

19 John Leland and Colin Moynihan. "Thousands March Silently to Protest Stop-and-Frisk Policies." *New York Times*, June 17, 2012. https://www.nytimes.com/2012/06/18/nyregion/thousands-march -silently-to-protest-stop-and-frisk-policies.html

20 Kyle Smith. "We Were Wrong About Stop and Frisk." *National Review*. January 1, 2018. https://www.nationalreview.com/2018/01 /new-york-city-stop-and-frisk-crime-decline-conservatives-wrong/

21 Rana Nazzal. Twitter post. August 14, 2014, 3:15 p.m. https:// twitter.com/rananazzalh/status/499997861669797888

22 Charlotte Alfred. "Protesters Say Ferguson Feels Like Gaza, Palestinians Tweet Back Advice." Huffington Post. Updated on August 15, 2014. https://www.huffpost.com/entry/ferguson -gaza_n_5679923

23 Sarah Dougherty. "Palestinians have some advice for the people of Ferguson, Missouri." The World. August 14, 2014. https://www.pri.org/stories/2014-08-14/palestinians-have-some-advice-people-ferguson-missouri

24 Alexis Goldstein. "Palestinians and Ferguson Protesters Link Arms Via Social Media." Yes! Solutions Journalism. August 16, 2014. https://www.yesmagazine.org/social-justice/2014/08/16/palestinians-and-ferguson-protesters-link-arms-via-social-media

25 Bassem Masri. "In Ferguson, I am reminded of Palestine." American Friends Service Committee. October 28, 2014. https://www.afsc.org/blogs/acting-in-faith/ferguson-i-am-reminded-palestine

26 Middle Easterner. Twitter post. October 31, 2014, 7:37 a.m. https://twitter.com/HouriaWaBas/status/528148702016192513

27 The National Archives Editors. "John Lewis - March from Selma to Montgomery, 'Bloody Sunday,' 1965." The National Archives. https://www.archives.gov/exhibits/eyewitness/html.php?section=2

28 Los Angeles Times Editors. "Selma 50 years later: Remembering Bloody Sunday." Los Angeles Times. March 6, 2015. https://www.youtube.com/watch?v=Vn6uQBDAr_U

29 History.com Editors. "Selma to Montgomery March." History.com. Updated on January 11, 2022. https://www.history.com/topics/black-history/selma-montgomery-march

30 Hidaya Foundation Editor. "What Does Hidaya Mean?" Hidaya Foundation. https://www.hidaya.org/about-us/what-does-hidaya-mean/

31 Linley Sanders. "What the Confederate flag means in America today." YouGovAmerica. January 13, 2020. https://today.yougov.com/topics/politics/articles-reports/2020/01/13/what-confederate-flag-means-america-today

32 Southern Poverty Law Center Editors. "Ku Klux Klan." Southern Poverty Law Center. https://www.splcenter.org/fighting-hate/extremist-files/ideology/ku-klux-klan

33 Richard E. Miller. "Midcity at the Crossroads." Spiritual Life Historical Marker. Shaw Heritage Trail. Page last revised December 22, 2021. https://www.hmdb.org/m.asp?m=130889

34 Katharine Q. Seelye. "John Lewis, Towering Figure of Civil Rights Era, Dies at 80." *New York Times*. Updated on August 4, 2020. https://www.nytimes.com/2020/07/17/us/john-lewis-dead.html

35 John P. Rafferty. "Women's March worldwide protest [2017]." Brittanica. Updated on January 14, 2022. https://www.britannica.com/event/Womens-March-2017

36 Tim Wallace and Alicia Parlapiano. "Crowd Scientists Say Women's March in Washington Had 3 Times as Many People as Trump's Inauguration." *New York Times*. Updated on January 22,

2017. https://www.nytimes.com/interactive/2017/01/22/us/politics
/womens-march-trump-crowd-estimates.html

37 Erica Chenoweth and Jeremy Pressman. "This is what we learned
by counting the women's marches." *Washington Post*. February 7,
2017. https://www.washingtonpost.com/news/monkey-cage/wp/2017
/02/07/this-is-what-we-learned-by-counting-the-womens-marches/

38 Joanna Walters and Amanda Holpuch. "Explainer: what is Daca
and who are the Dreamers?" *The Guardian*. June 18, 2020. https://
www.theguardian.com/us-news/2020/jun/18/daca-dreamers-us
-immigration-explainer

39 National Park Service Editors. "The New Colossus." National
Park Service. Accessed July 2021. https://www.nps.gov/stli/learn
/historyculture/colossus.htm

40 Hayes Gardner. "Breonna Taylor protesters want police in jail.
Instead, 435 of them have been arrested." *USA Today*. July 16, 2020.
https://www.usatoday.com/story/news/nation/2020/07/16/breonna
-taylor-protesters-arrests-show-we-mean-business/5453172002/

41 Billy Kobin. "Porsha Williams, Yandy Smith, more arrested at
Breonna Taylor protest: 'It was my pleasure.'" *USA Today*. July 15,
2020. https://www.usatoday.com/story/entertainment/celebrities
/2020/07/15/porsha-williams-yandy-smith-more-arrested-breonna
-taylor-protest/5442210002/

42 Richard A. Oppel Jr. and Kim Barker. "New Transcripts Detail Last Moments for George Floyd." *New York Times*. Updated on April 1, 2021. https://www.nytimes.com/2020/07/08/us/george -floyd-body-camera-transcripts.html

43 Chenoweth and Pressman. "Counting the Women's Marches."

44 Phyllis Bennis. "February 15, 2003. The Day the World Said No to War." Institute for Policy Studies. February 15, 2013. https://ips -dc.org/february_15_2003_the_day_the_world_said_no_to_war/

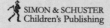

Throughout history, girls have often been discussed
in terms of what they couldn't or shouldn't do.
Not anymore.
It's time for *herstory*!